'The room was deafened with the blast of Kane's revolver, and only he heard the whistle of the knife sizzling an inch past his ear. It stuck quivering in the thick wooden frame of the door. The Breed was still standing, left hand splayed against the wall behind him, his face wide with an expectant grin of victory, his right arm following through after his throw to swing down at his side. Then his expression altered, and he gazed dumbstruck at the burnt hole in his coat. Something went to pieces inside his chest, and a flood of frothy pink fluid filled his mouth . . .'

U.S. Marshal Morgan Kane had come to Dakota territory to save lives, not to destroy them, but when a giant half-breed Indian like Charlie starts a fight then there's only one way to end it . . .

Also by Louis Masterson

WITHOUT MERCY
THE CLAW OF THE DRAGON
THE STAR AND THE GUN
BACKED BY THE LAW
A RANGER'S HONOUR
MARSHAL AND MURDERER
PISTOLERO
THE MONSTER FROM YUMA
THE DEVIL'S MARSHAL
GUNMAN'S INHERITANCE
REVENGE
STORM OVER SONORA
THE LAW OF THE JUNGLE
NO TEARS FOR MORGAN KANE
BETWEEN LIFE AND DEATH
RETURN TO ACTION
RIO GRANDE
BRAVADO
THE GALLOWS EXPRESS
RANSOM
KILLING FOR THE LAW
THE BUTCHER FROM GUERRERO
DUEL IN TOMBSTONE
TO THE DEATH, SENOR KANE!

Hell Below Zero

Louis Masterson

CORGI BOOKS
A DIVISION OF TRANSWORLD PUBLISHERS LTD

HELL BELOW ZERO

A CORGI BOOK 0 552 09526 5

First publication in Great Britain

PRINTING HISTORY

Corgi edition published 1974

Translated from the Norwegian by
Jeffrey M. Wallmann

This book is set in Times 10/10½ pt.

Corgi Books are published by Transworld Publishers Ltd.,
Cavendish House, 57–59 Uxbridge Road, Ealing,
London, W.5.

Made and printed in Great Britain by
Richard Clay (The Chaucer Press), Ltd., Bungay, Suffolk.

NOTE: The Australian price appearing on the back cover is the recommended retail price.

HELL BELOW ZERO

ONE

The Indian working his way down the snow slope was dressed in skins he'd prepared himself—wolfskin jacket, foxskin pants, and a cap of raccoon. On his back were the pelts of three foxes he'd already caught, and in his right hand he clutched a carbine. He was wearing snowshoes, and despite the surrounding shrubbery, he moved swift and sure.

He had a trap down along the riverbank, where the foxes ran, and the animals on his back had been caught farther up, just under the waterfall.

The Indian's name was Charlie Bowen, but he was called 'Three Crow'. He'd been a trapper for most of his life, the steel-toothed traps and strychnine capsules making his work easier for him now that he was getting on in years. He was nearly fifty, his wiry lean body hardened to the country, the cold, and the enormous distances he had to travel. Three Crow didn't know what a kilometer or a mile was, his range being measured in terms of day-marches. The least he could walk in one day was fifty kilometers. His horizon—becoming restricted even now, during his own generation—was endless.

North was Saskatchewan, Canada—interminable plains of countless lakes, bogs, and tundra.

South was the headwaters of the Missouri River, a giant lake spreading almost through North and South Dakota.

West was the Yellowstone River in Montana, the dizzying peaks, and the endless conifer forests.

East was the Red River prairie in Minnesota, and the black-smoking railroad which paralleled the river.

Within these borders was Three Crow's hunting grounds,

an enormous, wild region which the government called the Dakota Territory – Indian Territory.

The winter was Three Crow's working day, the animal tracks easy to follow and his snowshoes giving him wings. This was the season in which the fur was full and costly—beaver, fox, marten, muskrat, hare, wolf, and bear ... an endlessness of animals, from the elk and grizzly bear to the tiny snow mouse, not much larger than a hazelnut.

In the summer months the sky would drift and the rain would fall, and then Three Crow could smell the seasoning of pine and fir, and savor the rich tang of the marshlands. In the summer, he could rest, fish, and laze.

But the winter—when the northern lights flamed high over Turtle Mountain and the slender spruce creaked and groaned—the winter was his working day, and under the northern lights, the days were short.

Three Crow reached the bank of the river. Under a meter of snow and easily as much ice the water flowed, the stones in the riverbed creating mounds in the snow which cast blue shadows. Three Crow worked quickly through the loose snow, toward the tree where he'd set this particular trap.

When he came to the trap, he saw that while there were plenty of tracks around, the bait had been left untouched and the trap had not been sprung. He turned away, disappointed, but trying not to let it show.

He went on, climbing a hill until he came to a small plateau along the side ridge, and then he turned northward. It was a four-hour trek back to his cabin, which was cutting it close. In four hours, it would be nearly dark. He paused, tying the fox pelts together with a rawhide thong and slinging them over his back, and then putting on his rabbit-skin mittens, he began trudging the long way home.

The temperature had been thirty below zero when he'd started out that morning, and it hadn't warmed up appreciably since then. His breath hung white in front of him, and the snow groaned where the wind had piled it too high.

Three Crow continued plodding northward, through a narrow valley and past a dangerous overhang, following the frozen river toward a wide hill. Turtle Mountain appeared as a white gleam in the distance, an ivory pupil four thousand meters high in the eye of the red, glaring sunset.

The massive ridge loomed closer, grim and frozen in the stationary air, and Three Crow's breath was sticking like knives in his lungs before he reached its summit. Here he stood for a moment to rest, breathing into his mittens and noticing how the moisture froze instantly to ice. He shook himself slightly, getting the rigid fox carcasses to lay more comfortably, and then began to move down the other side of the hill.

The shadows were long and blue among the spruce by the time he came down to the sheltered valley where his cabin was. Instead of satisfaction as he approached, his eye was filled with dread. He saw smoke curling skyward between the majestic, thick spruce, and it was smoke that was oddly gray and sour-looking.

Had he forgotten to bank the fire before he'd left that morning?

No . . .

Then Three Crow was running, running as fast as he could, the snow cascading like a waterfall around his snowshoes. He followed the trail of smoke, knowing with fearful intuition that it was coming from his cabin. It was not the Indian's way to express desperation, but his lungs worked heavily, and the hissing which escaped from deep in his throat *could* have been a moaning . . .

He stopped beside the little marsh that bordered his cabin.

On the other side, his cabin rested on a low hillock, under the shade of an overhanging cliff.

Or rather, what was left of his cabin . . .

The framework and walls of split logs were sunk around the low foundation wall, smoking and glowing, occasionally spitting into crackling flame. Only the stone fireplace still remained, pointing like a blackened finger heavenward as if in accusation . . .

Three Crow tossed the foxes into the snow and ran frantically across the marsh to the ruins. He circled helplessly, seeing it was totally destroyed, and beyond the smoldering embers were the burnt leftovers of his cached skins—a half-winter's trappings! Everything he owned was gone—food, tools, weapons, *everything.*

How could it have happened? Had it started somehow from the fireplace, a rolling log perhaps falling onto the floor...? But it was a stone floor, and he had carefully covered the fire with earth before leaving! It didn't make any sense!

And what of his dogs? Where were they?

He whistled, sharply.

The sound disappeared between the spruce. The only answer was a sudden, sharp snap of a tree grown too cold. The sun had almost entirely disappeared behind the mountain ridge now, and the frigidity was seeping into Three Crow's bones as he stood impatiently waiting for his dogs to bark, just as it had gotten into the limbs of the tree. He snorted like a furious bear, and again circled around the ruins of his cabin, his face stern and hard. A few minutes later his keen eyes had perceived what had happened here—two men had visited after he'd left that morning. Two men, and the cabin had burnt down in an hour or two, dry as it was.

Two men!

What had they done? Had they gone inside for shelter, kindled the fire and forgotten to bank it when they'd gone again? Had a sudden wind produced too great a draft in the chimney, causing the fire to become so raging it had caught the woodpile beside the hearth? No ... No, there hadn't been any wind this day.

In the final rays of daylight he investigated further. Abruptly he saw a slight wink of light, and stooping, he saw that the light had reflected off two cartridge casings left in the debris. They still smelled of gunpowder, the carbon left on the shells smudging his mittens when he picked them up to examine them.

Someone had been shooting—at what?

Once again he toured the cabin foundations, and shortly he discovered the tracks of his dogs. He followed them, and soon he found Delaware, his white and gray husky. The dog was sprawled out with its jaw grimaced and its eyes frozen shut, and there was blood covering its fur and surrounding snow. A little farther on was the whelp, shot through the head. Its brains were a startling, contrasting pink to the whiteness, and as he stared in grief, Three Crow recalled an incident from many years before. He had fought a shaven-headed Huron along Lake Erie, and had sunk his axe into the other's skull, and now he remembered how surprised he'd been at the color which had bubbled out of the wound...

It was getting too dark to continue investigating, and the cold was laming his feet. He went around the cabin one last time, trying to find something of value, something of his to retrieve or something of the men's as a clue, but he found nothing. And as the last glowing embers began to die out, he started jumping up and down, both to keep warm and to vent his frustrated rage.

He had three fox skins, his carbine, matches, ammunition, and the clothes on his back. That was all.

And it was a good three days' march to Dawson's trading post.

Three Crow looked at the remains of his home for a final moment. Then, with a threatening gesture with his gun, he pivoted around and started the long way southward.

The moonlight was treacherous. Shadows which normally indicated roughness were now whispered away, and only years of living in the savage land and a habit of carefulness saved the Indian from bad spills that night. And to trip could mean a sprained or broken limb, and such an injury would mean ultimate death. He traveled by way of his closest traps in hopes that they'd have snared an animal he could eat, but he discovered they were all empty. His luck remained bad.

Revenge festered in Three Crow, deeply ingrained from when he'd been a young warrior. He'd taken his first scalp at the age of fifteen, at a time when his tribe's feuding had ravaged the Dakotas, and now the thought of vengeance kept him warm and determined. The certainty that he'd be able to track the murderers kept him alive and pointed forward. It was only the knowledge that he had to reach Dawson's post in order to survive that kept him from chasing the men now without food or equipment. The rest of the winter would have to be spent in trapping, to pay back Dawson for any credit given now, but then those two murderers would find an old wolf dogging their trail.

Three Crow called the men 'murderers' not just because they'd killed his dogs. By burning him out in the middle of winter, they'd done their best to murder him too.

But despite the hate and the revenge that burned in his heart, the pain in his legs told Three Crow there was little chance of reaching Dawson's alive. It was too far and too cold, and he had too little to make it...

When finally the weather stiffened his legs like tree limbs, he found himself a small spot in a snowdrift piled against a spruce scrub. He removed his snowshoes and used them to dig a hole close to their trunks, and then sheltered, he wormed out his matches. He sat and brooded over his tiny fire the rest of the night, unable to remove the cold in his body. He hadn't eaten anything for a whole day, and he was dreaming of a big slab of meat as he stared at the fragile flames before him. He envisioned his fireplace and the blackened pan which hung on a nail beside it, the heavy pan that was always greased and ready to use on such a slice of meat. He thought of how the meat bulged out at first and got red as the blood oozed out and mixed with the sauce; then it would get a light brown, and then a darker brown, the sizzling odor spreading under the low ceiling...

The dream broke and he snapped awake, the heat from his small fire singeing his face. Darkly, he threw a few more pieces of wood on and hoped the day would soon appear...

Three Crow had gone without food before, and for days on end. But then he'd been young and the blood that was tepid in his flesh had been full of fire. Now the blood pumped sluggishly and his limbs weren't as maleable, so willing to obey his brain. It wasn't fair, he thought disgustedly, not for an old man like him...

Eventually it began to lighten among the spruce with approaching dawn, and Three Crow wearily put on his snowshoes again. He covered the still burning campfire with snow and then set off southward. It was colder than it had been the day before, and he never felt a bit of warmth in his feet again. There was the ever-present danger of frost-bite, closer now in his weakened condition, but his only chance lay in them moving.

Go feet, he muttered to them. *Are you hearing? Go, feet, and get yourself warm ...*

His feet reluctantly stirred. Faintly they carried him over the frozen expanse, across the marshy land and through the sparse trees and along the gnarled ridges and over lakes which had blue glimpses of ice where the wind had swept the snow away.

It was on the outskirts of one such lake that he heard the wolves for the first time. The chilling howls sliced through his marrow and bone. He had long since discarded the fox carcasses, refusing to take chances that he might be poisoned by them, and he hoped that the wolves would linger over them, should they be following his trail. But then, perhaps they were not; perhaps they had just spotted him and were closing in without knowing about the deadly foxes. And the cold in his feet and the fatigue in his muscles and the burning in his eyes, it was all draining him, killing him just as surely, if more slowly. And the wolves were coming, he could hear them louder now, low and quick, with their muzzles clinging to the scent ...

The red February sun slowly rose over the highest of the mountain ridges, and then began the descent into darkness once again. Three Crow held a steady, determined course, refusing to admit defeat or the closeness of the wolves. He was able to reach the mouth of a river before nightfall, before he was afraid to go farther. He stopped where he discovered a small amount of wood almost hidden in the snow, and breaking the branches into kindling, he was able to get another fire going.

But no matter how high the flames snapped, or how close he sat, he was unable to stop the cold from creeping deeper inside of him. At this point, he was not even able to see the imaginary piece of meat while he was poking the fire; he was only able to envisage smoking, cooling ruins, and the bodies of two dead dogs.

He heard a snap close by, and had to force himself to

turn around. His carbine was placed close to the fire, where the heat would melt the frigid gun-oil. He removed one mitten and quickly put his bare hand under his coat, inside the pocket where he kept his cartridges. There were twelve of them, all he ever needed when tending his traps. Just a dozen . . . and now he was beginning to wish the wolves would come, to make his bullets eleven, and to add a warm dead furry body and possibly some stringy meat to his possessions . . .

He slept for a moment beside the fire, lifting his head suddenly when he felt as though he were being watched. He raised his rifle, seeing the low shadows slinking away between the snowdrifts. The sharp, cold shot sounded dry and absurd as it chased itself across the flattened lake and hit the black mountain beyond to come echoing back. The gunsmoke was acrid and pungent in his nose.

But just by firing, he'd cheered himself up. He was still alive, still game and fighting, and with a weapon.

But they were still out there, more than a dozen it seemed, outside the reflection of the firelight. He saw the quick gleam of yellow-green eyes, the shadowy forms snaking in and out faster than he could aim. He stoked the fire angrily and greedily drank the melting snow. It was a long, bitter night for the weakening Indian.

The chill is at its worst in the morning, but the wolves were gone as ghosts with the first rays of light. Three Crow jumped and danced in an effort to unlimber his body, and he had to try three times before he could bend over and put on his snowshoes. One time he fell flat in the snow, and that scared him worse than the look of the wolves as they'd glared at him.

He forced his body to carry him again, crawling heavily upward, past the inlet of the river, and all the way to the top of the next ridge. The sun slid slowly across the spruce, redder than the blood in his veins.

One more day's walking, he thought. No, two. He hadn't gone fast enough, far from fast enough. He went down the ridge, and in the late morning he began to hear the barks behind him once again.

No . . . wolves don't give up easily, if at all . . .

Almost weaving, his arms and legs feeling like rubber to him, Three Crow staggered on through a dense growth of briars and scrub, coming at last to a low-lying stretch of frozen marshland.

The marsh was a familiar landmark to the Indian, its birch-brush, willow, and grassy knolls stretching west of Devil's Lake in what was to become North Dakota. During the summer, the marsh swarmed with geese, ducks, partridge, quail, and hosts of wading birds. In the autumn the hunters would come, to be swallowed up by the enormous stretches until they couldn't see one another, but only hear occasional shots crack like tinder across the vastness.

Three Crow stopped and searched, digging through the snow and hardened bog until he discovered a nest of dormant mice. He ate them alive, crunching their tiny bones between his teeth, having to eat something, something to give him strength and warmness. The wolves were very close now, and he could make out nine of them in an uneven row as they covertly approached. He turned his back to them and searched for another small burrow, eating the febril rodents as fast as he uncovered them. A couple of times he was close to gagging on them, but he forced himself to keep the raw food down.

He moved on, hurriedly now. Before, he'd always been able to cross the marsh in one day, but now he had no choice. He *had* to cross it and be inside the woods on the opposite shore before dark, before it became too late to start another fire.

But the day was late for him to be starting such a journey, the sun rolling red-eyed on the rim of the surrounding hills. Parts of the marsh were already becoming etched in shadow, and the pack of wolves were growing with the afternoon, pulling closer with the dusk. He had to keep them somehow at bay.

He stripped one mitten off, levering the carbine and feeling its icy metal stab through his skin. Savagely he whirled and sent two shots into the pack behind him.

The sound reverberated across the marsh.

The wolves crouched very still, staring malevolently at him.

He lowered the carbine, knowing he'd failed to scare them, much less hit one. Two cartridges spoilt. But the sudden noise and the black-powder smell cheered him, seeming to speed him on again.

But he wasn't moving faster, not really, and he knew deep inside him that the voice of his soul was right. The marsh would be his grave.

No . . . No!

No, by the Spirit, those wolves would be empty of belly tonight as he!

He waved his arms violently for circulation as he stumbled on. The shadows lengthened, the white ridge ahead turning slowly to a light, hazy blue . . . then a darker blue . . . then almost a black . . . His eyes were swollen and painful from lack of sleep at night and the glare of snow by day. How far, how far was it again? Didn't the ridge rise soon? It must, it must . . .

The cold had left his feet now. They were numb, no longer a part of him. He rubbed his legs through the skin-tight pants, and then drove on. The wolves held their distance with the patience of vultures—perhaps a hundred meters behind—nine killer animals with bushy tails and triangular faces and gray-black muzzles of muscled jaw and sharpened fang. Their bitter eyes hung on the man who moved so strangely, who zig-zagged in staggering steps, who thrust himself toward the dark mountain ridge.

The Indian stopped. His lungs were like open wounds and his arms were stiffening, tingling with pin-pricks of pain. His raccoon cap creaked with ice, and his wolfskin jacket had long icicles along the chest where he'd been dribbling. He noticed that his cheeks were hard as stone; he'd forgotten to rub them. He could hardly move his fingers when he tried.

Again he measured the distance to the forested ridge.

He'd never make it.

But Three Crow refused to capitulate, or even whine. He sat down in the snow with his carbine across his knees, feeling weary and discouraged. The wolves sat down too, watching him, always watching him. Three Crow watched the darkness creep over the bog, and it was too cold for tears to form in his eyes. He sat and watched, and listened to his inner voice, the voice that whispered insistently that the murderers had killed more than two dogs...

Came the dawn, and Three Crow was still sitting in the same position, his rifle across his knees and his face turned toward the wolves. The pack stirred uneasily, shaking the snow from their fur. Why didn't the man get up, too? Why wasn't he going on as before?

Slowly they prowled nearer, until the leader wolf saw the eyes in the ashen-marble face. They were dead eyes, without any gleam or warmth to them. The leader paused, then leaped forward...

TWO

'Thirty below,' the conductor called out. 'Watch your step!'

Morgan Kane jumped from the train to the platform and looked around the small town of Fargo. Snowdrifts were piled high on either side of the tracks, and in the early light of morning, only a few low log houses were visible. A sudden spark from a nearby chimney made Kane long for a warm place, a bed, and a decent meal. He started along the platform in search of them, the snow and ice squeaking miserably under his boots.

He walked along the main street, past the station yard, a couple of dogs barking at him as he went. What they were doing out in weather like this was beyond him. Fargo was just another line-town beside the railway. Timber was its livelihood, and by the looks of the large, jutting planks beneath the mounds of snow, there was plenty of it. The Red River ran on the east side of the town, silently now and blanketed with a thick layer of ice, resembling the naked, frozen bogs which bordered its banks. Kane's cheeks were beginning to feel like the bogs, and his toes were gluing themselves to the leather and two pairs of woolen socks around them.

It was damned cold!

Something resembling a hotel came into view. It was a couple of floors with a few kerosene lanterns strung across the porch entrance. The rosy flames from the lanterns cast a pitiful light across the snow. Nearing, Kane saw there was a sign hanging from the porch roof, beaded with ice, and vaguely through the ice he could make out the faded letters:

Kane went inside. A pot-belly stove snapped at itself in the corner, its cast iron redder than the lanterns had been outside. The head of a snarling grizzly hung on the wall beside it, flanked by two enormous elk antlers. They, if nothing else, told Kane he was about as far north as he could get.

'Howdy, bub,' a voice greeted.

Kane turned to face a heavily bearded man who'd entered the parlor from an inner door. The man was thickly dressed in a sweater and woolen pants and boots that seemed to be fashioned of strips of animal hide.

'I need a room,' Kane said. 'And breakfast.'

The man nodded, walking behind a counter and turning the registration book around to face Kane. 'Sign in,' he said, extending a pen. 'You planning to stay awhile?'

'Nope.' Kane scratched his name with frigid fingers. 'I'm going to head on west tomorrow, I think, to Dawson's.'

'Uh-huh. That'll be three bucks—in advance.' The clerk glanced at Kane's single leather bag, which was quite small. 'That's all you've got along, Mr, ah ... Kane?'

'Yeah.'

The man shrugged and took a key from one of the hooks on the pigeon-hole board behind him. 'Number 12, upstairs and to your right.'

Kane tramped up the steps and found his room. It was almost as cold inside it as it'd been out in the snow. But there was a small stove with a box of kindling and bark beside it, and soon Kane had a fire going in the grate. While the room was warming, he went to the window and looked outside.

The sun was up now, crimson and clear over the distant hills. For a moment, Kane felt almost as if he could peer into the forests that covered those hills, down where the elk pawed the marshes and swung their antlers from side to side, and the animals which didn't hibernate slunk through valleys in search of food. He could all but smell the campfires beneath the spruce, and hear the dogs howling and digging around the light, and the trees groaning under their weight of ice and snow...

Then the moment was gone, and he took off his jacket and coat and spread his hands close to the stove. He reminded himself to keep his revolver handy in his coat pocket from now on, and that deadly thought brought him immediately back to here and now.

U.S. Marshal Morgan Kane stood in front of the stove and shivered with cold, the cold which had built up inside of him during the long trip northward to the Dakota Territory. It had been a grueling, boring trip, with little to do but stare out at the frozen landscape during the days, and dream of Kate Coleman during the long nights.

Kate was never far from his thoughts. He'd met the red-haired temperamental journalist in Tombstone while closing in on a vicious gang of outlaws, and their romance had flared hot and tumultuous ever since. Their fights were frequent and furious, with a wildness that would've exhausted other couples—but their reconciliations were just as hot, hot and passionate and bittersweet.

When Kane wasn't thinking of Kate Colman on his trip, he reviewed the events in Shane's office of the Union Ranch, Fort Leavenworth. It had been a blustery day, the snow drifting high between the buildings, and the meeting had been short and terse. There, Kane had greeted two men from Washington—one from the Office of Indian Affairs, and the other from the Territorial Commission.

The man from the Indian Affairs Office was named Jefferson, and was a small, brown-skinned fellow—surprisingly so to Kane, who considered all office workers pale, flabby, and myopic. The other was younger, but with steel-rimmed glasses and the beginnings of a pot belly, and who more nearly fit Kane's preconceptions.

'Marshal,' Jefferson told Kane, 'What Mr Shane means is that you're the only one who can help us.'

Kane, who'd been sitting, stared along the bridge of his nose, not saying anything in reply. What could he say?

'We've been having considerable trouble in the Dakota Territory,' Jefferson continued, 'including the Royal Canadian Mounted Police.'

Kane had a quick vision of men dressed in red jackets,

polished boots, and ridiculously pointed hats, as Jefferson cleared his throat and went on.

'Briefly, we're talking about the land between Devil's Lake in the south, Garrison Lake in the west, and the Red River in the east; the traditional hunting grounds for the local tribes. There's been considerable fighting and killing in the district, enough so that Governor Meyer in Bismark has requested aid.'

'What's the trouble over?'

'It's not at all clear, other than somebody is attempting to force the Indians off the land on both sides of the border. A damned sad state of affairs, especially as the Canadian authorities are keen on keeping their Indians at peace. They seem to have gotten the impression that our policies are a great deal to blame for the disturbances, but of course, that's prepostrous. Hm. But enough of that. The point is, Governor Meyer has asked for Federal assistance, and after giving it considerable thought, we've decided to send a marshal up there first, to report what exactly is going on. Then we can decide what to do, but we must have the facts first.'

Kane glanced from Jefferson to Shane, unable to understand why he instead of an Indian Affairs representative should be picked. Shane seemed to read his mind, saying:

'It's a tough land up there, Morgan. Washington needs its clerks.'

His smile took the sting from his words, but Jefferson still looked mildly insulted. They both turned their attention to Kane, waiting for his answer. It would be a choiceless answer; Kane didn't have any wild desire to travel to the north country, but this was his assignment now, and it was his duty to go where sent. By putting the order in the form of a request, it was made a little more palatable—but not much.

'Okay,' Kane agreed with a heavy sigh. 'Immediately?'

'Immediately—if not before,' Jefferson replied, rising.

Hands were shook, and Jefferson wished Kane the best of luck before leaving the office. Then, when the door was closed again, Shane said: 'Well, you always wanted a raccoon cap, Morgan. Here's your chance.'

Kane smiled thinly. 'I'll remember that.'

Shane opened a desk drawer, removing some reports, a train schedule, and a map. 'Looks like the train goes as far as Fargo,' he said, stretching the map out on the desk top. 'From there it's another thirty miles to Dawson's Trading Post, which is the center for the local trappers. I suggest you start there . . .'

The way to Dawson's was northwesterly, over a wide and trampled road. The four steaming horses made the trip in half a day, and Kane—who sat in the back of an open-bed wagon—was glad he'd put on everything he had along. He knew Dakota was cold in the winter, but even so the primitive intensity of it surprised him. It was the vast distances, the ever-stretching mountains and lakes that overcame him—it was a country of paths and teamsters, not streets and railroads.

The sun was brushing the high horizon by the time his wagon pulled up to Dawson's. The trading post was little more than a group of timber cabins beside a frozen lake, which in turn hugged the jutting hills. Tracks of wagons, sleds, men, and dogs spread out in all directions. Two of the buildings were obviously stables, evident by the stacks of hay covered by tarps near their wide barn doors. On the snow-covered courtyard were dogs lying like dark spots, taking over the horses' role during the winter season.

'Dawson's, mister!' the wagon driver said to Kane.

Kane climbed down stiffly, grasping his leather case, and started for the head building as the driver moved on toward the closer stable. The main building was a single storey high, with three chimneys belching gray smoke into the clear, cold air. Kane kicked the ice from his boots on the steps, seeing a pair of snowshoes leaning against the side of the stairs.

Seeing them reminded the Marshal of when he'd first tried learning how to use the fool contraptions. It'd been in Oregon, and he'd been tempted several times to throw them in the fire and make some use of them, the technique of walking in them not one easily learned. Smiling at the memory, he opened the door and stepped inside, and was greeted by the burning breath of smoke and the pungent odor of sweat.

The light inside cast the frozen windows into sharp, sparkling relief. The light mostly came from two open hearths at either end of the long room, huge pine stumps burning in them with a yellowish kind of crackling flame. There was a long bar beside one of the fireplaces, and beyond that were a number of tables and benches.

At first, the room seemed densely populated with a race of giants, and the massive tables and benches looked dwarfed under the crowd of fur-clad mastodons. It took a while before Kane discovered that the initial impression was mostly due to the massive jackets the men were wearing. But they were still large and brawny, sitting as they did in boisterous groups, laughing and roaring and sucking on pipes that stunk like sweet hell. The walls were decorated with skins and antlers and heads—trophies of the hunt—some of them the largest Kane had ever seen.

A couple of the men turned when Kane entered, and seeing it was a stranger, they nudged their neighbors. Soon it was silent in the room as everybody stared, and then one of the men began to snort, another laughed, and then they all began to laugh in good-natured derision. It would have been the same if one of these skin-dressed brutes had wandered into the Oriental Saloon in Tombstone.

Kane waited for the first bellows to die down and then said: 'Is there a skin rug to spare? My feet are about frozen off.'

That started the laughter again, but two more men waved for him to join them. 'This here should curl you to your toenails, Stranger!' one of them hooted. 'Try a Dawson Special!'

Kane went over and sat down. He took off his gloves and blew on his hands until he was able to reach for the large iron mug they offered. The unshaven faces leered at him, as if curious to see if he could stomach the contents.

Kane held his breath when he took a swallow. He managed to get the liquor down without wincing despite his stomach turning suddenly inside out, but he couldn't stop a couple of tears rolling from his eyes. Gritting his teeth, he held out the mug.

'Now how about one for my other foot?'

The man laughed good-naturedly at this, refilling his cup.

The second slug dropped like a silver dollar to meet the first. 'Ahhh,' Kane gasped in a whispered voice. 'That's good. Is Dawson around?'

One of the men waved with his pipe. 'In his office, counting his money out to Swan. He brought in forty pelts yesterday.'

'But Swan drank up ten of them already,' another said.

'Yah, and owed twenty from last season.'

'So he has ten left, if he is lucky.'

Kane took out his tobacco pouch and rolled a cigarette. After he'd lit it, he found that he had warmed up enough to take off his coat. The men stared suspiciously at his dark suit.

'You must freeze in that,' the man on his right grunted.

'Yeah, almost have already,' he replied.

'You planning to hunt in them duds?'

'I'm not here to hunt. I'm just looking around.'

Suddenly the friendliness was gone, the stares and expressions cold, hard, and distant. 'Should have guessed,' a black-bearded gent snarled. 'Just like them dudes in Washington dress in.'

'I'm not from Washington,' Kane replied calmly. 'But what if I am?'

The bearded man leaned forward. 'We don't like being told how to live, Stranger. If that's on your mind, you better high-tail it outa here before that wagon of yours goes back to Fargo.

Kane drew on his cigarette, letting the smoke filter through his nostrils. 'There've been men here who've tried to do that?'

'For damned sure. Dudes from Bismark with bowler hats and patent leather shoes. Gov'ment men, never seen a grizzly outside a museum, or a fox skin on anything except a lady.'

'And they tried to tell you how to live?'

'Uh-huh. Lotta nonsense about responsibility; about the day coming when this here will be a State and we have to be prudent and responsible. You should've seen the last dude here, how responsible and prudent he was after Clyde sicced his dogs after him.'

Kane laughed. 'Well, I'm not from the Governor in Bismark,' he said. 'Nor from Washington. I'm here to classify the plants and animals, a lot of which aren't found anywhere else in the Union.'

'Huh?'

'You mean you is one of them there scientist fellers?'

'A, a zoo-ologist?' a third one said.

'Call it how you please,' the first one snorted. 'It's collecting a bunch of ferns and things and pressing them in school.'

'Maybe they're doing that in school nowadays,' Kane answered with a smile, 'but you can't squeeze a fox that way.'

'Or a squaw,' the bearded one chuckled. 'You here to collect a couple of Indian squaws too, Stranger?'

They all roared with laughter.

Kane looked at them, wondering for a moment if he should tell them the truth. If they wanted to know more about his supposed profession of nature-hunting, he'd soon be discovered as a phony. Besides, he had the job of collecting what he was really here for—information—and he had to start somewhere.

He pounded his fist on the table, and when he'd gotten their undivided attention, he said seriously: 'Listen, I'll spit it out for you. I'm Morgan Kane, and I'm a U.S. Marshal.'

Dozens of eyes glared ruthlessly at him. 'What the hell do you want with us?' one of them hissed.

'Bounty hunting?' another jibed.

'Only things we skin around here are animals,' a third snapped, 'so the fine ladies of New York won't freeze their keesters.'

'I'm here about the Indians,' Kane said quietly. 'About the Indians who're being driven from their lands and being murdered.'

It was very, very quiet.

Kane raised his voice. 'Does anybody here know anything about it?'

Again, not a sound, hardly a movement.

Kane searched the sullen, bitter expressions surrounding him. Out of the corner of his eye he caught the movement of two men who'd been sitting in a corner till now, separated from the others. While the others were still, they were inching forward, as if ready to attack. Kane turned to face them, to study them carefully.

One would have stood out anywhere. He was a Breed, rawboned and angular with massive shoulders which jutted out his fur jacket. Black greasy hair dangled down over his forehead, but only partially covered a flaming scar across his brow. The puckered wound ran down against his left ear, a momento of a knifing which had sliced his forehead and left the skin hanging down over his eyes.

The other man didn't look quite so horrible, so frighteningly savage, but he was a giant. A dark, bushy-haired giant, with the features of a French-Canadian. It was this man who finally broke the silence, speaking to Kane in a peculiar singing dialect.

'The only ones who have forced the Indians away have been your men, Marshal, Government men. Charlie, he can tell you. You see his scar, eh? It came from a Government sword, south of Black Hills.'

The half-Indian called Charlie stood up with ponderous anger, his face stoic and yet burning underneath with ill-disguised hatreds. At once Kane knew that his own life was hanging by a very, very thin thread.

THREE

A deathly quiet settled over the room, broken only by the occasional sparks snapping in the fireplace.

'You should curb your dog, Laverne,' a gruff voice said behind Kane. 'Yes, sir, I'd say you should.'

It was a spontaneous comment coming out of seemingly nowhere, but Kane instantly recognized that this was the pretext which Charlie needed—and was going to use! The Breed's eyes smouldered with sudden fury.

'So, I'm a dog, eh?' he snarled at Kane.

Kane quietly replied: 'I didn't say that.'

'No, *you* don't have to. *You* just look at me that way, without the hair to come out and admit it. You're nothing but a yellow gov'ment man, and that's enough for me. When I finish with you, mister, the women folk will turn around and shiver!'

Kane noticed Laverne leaning smugly against the wall, his thick brown arms crossed lackadaisically, as if pleased with the prospect of the Breed beating Kane to a pulp. Kane's eyes darted back to the grimacing Charlie, and saw there was no way to avoid a confrontation; he peeled off his coat, but his right arm was still in the bulky sleeve when Charlie hit him the first time. It was a solid punch, and it flung Kane down and across the floor, skidding him under the long table. The men sitting there knocked him mercilessly with their boots, forcing him out from under and into Charlie's reach again—not because they had anything particularly against him, but because he was a stranger they didn't trust and had yet to prove his merit.

Kane threw his coat off and rose just in time to avoid a gruesome kick to the head. He back-pedaled, regaining his breath and swerving away from Charlie's long arms.

'Yallar bastard!' the Breed snarled.

Kane didn't respond to the insult, saving his breath as he circled around, ducking from the heavily swinging fists. He saw an opening and abruptly darted in to hit a quick one-two into Charlie's belly. It was like thumping a brick wall, Charlie's fur coat and muscled torso absorbing his blows as if they'd never existed. Charlie laughed, once, sharply, and walloped back, and Kane was sent staggering all the way back into the fireplace wall. The pain was acute in his chest; he wondered if a rib had been cracked or broken.

Charlie moved in with confidence, and Kane feinted with a low thrust, then threw a right fist upwards into the scarred face. It wiped the smile off Charlie's mouth, snapping his head back, but his eyes didn't even blink, remaining implacable with hatred. It had been a Sunday punch, yet hadn't even fazed the Breed, and Kane began to feel the first tendrils of fear. He'd heard about men like this—met a few, though never fought them before—who could take any kind of punishment and dish it back twice as hard. Before Kane might be able to knock Charlie out, he could be beaten senseless himself—perhaps even killed!

'You weasel shit,' Charlie sneered contemptuously, and threw himself at Kane. 'I've had women slap me harder than that!'

Kane ducked away from the burly arms and then suddenly pivoted around and came in close again. Charlie, off balance, was wide open with his chin stuck out and exposed; Kane straightened, butting his skull against that chin with all the power of his neck and shoulders. Teeth smacked together and Charlie's shaggy head whipped back as if his spine had been broken, but almost in automatic reflex, he wrapped his arms around Kane in a bear hug. He squeezed murderously, crushing Kane's already bruised ribs, tightening his hold and chuckling while he heard Kane's breath gurgling from straining lungs.

Kane wriggled in Charlie's hug, fearing he'd be snapped in two at this rate. He butted his head a second time, this time down against the hawk-like beak of Charlie's nose. A stream of blood spasmed from Charlie's nostrils, rivuleting down his face like red tears to stain his fur coat. His grip loosened slightly, and his beady eyes became filled with water. Kane sent his boots hard against the Breed's shins, bashed his nose another time ... and Charlie let go in spasmodic pain.

'I'll kill you for this!' Charlie raged, rubbing his swollen nose with the back of his hand and staring furiously at the blood. 'I'll kill you deader than a poop!'

Kane warily circled, breathing harshly. His right hand felt numb and stiff, fingers like long lead weights. He parried a wild roundhouse and danced backwards to avoid a flying kick, and desperate now with the knowledge it could not continue this way, he kicked back. His toe connected sweetly with Charlie's groin.

The Breed squeaked in a high voice and folded like a hinge, both hands clutching between his injured thighs.

'That was a good one,' one of the men hooted.

Charlie rushed Kane, his face white and furious except for his scar, which was a throbbing violet. Kane had to take three heavy swings before he finally connected with Charlie's broken nose again, and the blood gushed like a crimson fountain. Charlie backed away for the first time, shaking his head as if to clear a buzzing in his ears, and Kane, sensing this could be his final opportunity, drove against him. He hit Charlie across the throat with the solid edge of his hand, a chop to the adam's apple which was followed by a left fist to the temple. Charlie staggered sideways, hawking and spitting and holding his throat.

Kane hit him again, slashing another right to his neck the instant Charlie dropped his hand. The Breed cried out, a terrible curdled scream of hate, staggering in a half-crouch while he sucked for air and clawed for Kane. The Marshal straightened him with a savage uppercut, pounded him in the solar plexus four times, and bashed him in the nose and both eyes. Charlie lurched against the wall, dazed and defeated, and slowly slid down to sprawl in a sitting position on the floor.

Kane backed away, close to falling over himself. The room tilted before his eyes, reeling around feverishly while he willed his body to hold him upright. After a few moments he staggered toward the table where he'd dropped his coat. The humming was loud in his ears, and he wasn't sure if somebody called out to him or if it was the facial expressions of the men which warned him—but suddenly alarmed, he pivoted around.

Charlie, one hand braced against the wall, was back on his feet with death in his eyes. He was holding his large skinning knife in his right hand, aiming it straight for Kane. Kane pawed for his revolver, stuck in the waistband of his pants. The Breed threw the knife, and Kane leaped to one side, snapping two quick shots off.

The room was deafened with smoke and the blast of Kane's revolver, and only he heard the whistle of the knife sizzling an inch past his ear. It stuck quivering in the thick wooden frame of the door. The Breed was still standing, left hand splayed against the wall behind him, his face wide with an expectant grin of victory, his right arm following through after his throw to swing down at his side. Then his expression altered, and he gazed dumbstruck at the burnt hole in his coat. Something went to pieces inside his chest, and a flood of frothy pink fluid filled his mouth, dribbling down his chin to spatter the floor. He turned, frowning with disbelief, scratching the wall with his fingers, trying to say something, perhaps that it was a mistake, that no, he really didn't have to die this way, now . . .

Kane stood with his smoking gun, grimly following Charlie's death struggle while nausea welled up in his throat. He watched sickened as Charlie worked his jaw, valiantly trying to scream, but his voice was throttled in his burst lungs. Charlie crumpled to his knees, then holding his stomach, crashed over to lie still on the bloody planking.

Kane returned his revolver to his waistband, shaking his head.

'Don't, Laverne!' snapped a voice nearby.

Kane swiveled and saw Laverne behind him, his hand conveniently inside his coat as if reaching for a weapon.

The man who'd spoken continued menacingly: 'Charlie quarreled and got his rightfully. I've never denied you admission here before, but you ain't back-shooting nobody. You'd better get; you're not welcome here no more, Laverne. Don't you forget it.'

Laverne dropped his sneaking hand and rose, a spiteful glare directed at Kane. He snatched up his cap and clamped it tightly on his head, then stomped out of the post without a word.

Kane looked at the man who'd ordered Laverne out, figuring it was pretty obvious the guy had to be Dawson, the owner. Dawson was a hulking male over six foot, bulging of muscle, and dressed in a suit of deerskin, decorated with fringe.

'Thanks,' Kane said.

'Like I told Laverne, Charlie got what was coming. And it's been coming a long time. But who the hell are you, anyway?'

'Some fancy-dan sheriff from the south o' here,' another man answered before Kane had a chance to speak.

'He can talk for hisself,' Dawson snapped. 'Hank, get him a drink; he looks a mite peaked. And you, Sam, and Milt, haul Charlie's carcass outa here. Make sure the dogs don't get him.'

A couple of men began dragging the bloody corpse from the room, while a third—ostensibly Hank—poured Kane a shot-glass of whiskey from an unlabeled bottle. Kane swallowed the drink in one grateful gulp—then felt tears welling in his eyes. The booze seemed to have been distilled from Mexican chili peppers.

'Sit down,' Dawson said, and stepping further into the light, Kane could see that his face was badly mauled, probably by a wild animal some time before. 'Now, I asked you who you were,' he said when Kane had seated himself at the table. 'The word seems to be you're a lawman. Got proof?'

'Yes.' Kane showed him his star.

'A mite way from your home, ain't you, Marshal?' Dawson asked conversationally, and studied the revolver butt sticking up from Kane's waistband. 'And mighty handy with your iron, too.'

'But not so good with a blade,' Kane replied easily, thumbing toward the knife still buried in the door frame.

Dawson rubbed his massive jaw. 'Few are as good as Charlie was. What brings you here to my post?'

Kane paused, thinking how he should answer, and then figured to hell with it, he'd lay it on the line. 'The Indians here are being forced off their land. I want to know why.'

Dawson's eyes blazed momentarily. 'You've got guts, Marshal, coming in here and saying it flat out. What the hell, I'll tell you what I can—but I'm warning you, you squirrel around with us, and you're liable to end up skinned like a fox, your pelt hung up to dry.'

'I'm not after hides,' Kane chuckled with more humor than he felt. 'Least-ways, not two-legged variety. I'm after the truth, that's all. You play fair, and I'll play fair.'

Dawson massaged his jaw again, as if sizing up Kane. Finally he nodded, saying: 'All right, I'll string along. Fact is, there's been some odd happenings around here lately, and they've been sort of bothering me.'

'When did they start?'

'Long about last autumn, just after the ice began. First I heard of it was when three Crow Indians from Cheyenne River north of here suddenly up and died mysteriously. They were found in their canoe, frozen fast to the ice, and the wolves had been eating on them. It weren't a matter of drowning, because they were still in their canoe, but they weren't shot either, best we could tell. Looked like they'd plumb run out of food and supplies, but them Crows are a wily bunch, and that don't seem to make much sense. Then awhile later, close to Christmas, Benny Crow was found in his cottage; fire was out and he was like an icicle, and if you'd known Benny Crow, you'd have known it was a damned odd way for him to die. During January and February it happened several more times—other Indians disappearing or having strange accidents that were always fatal.'

'So everybody was curious,' Kane said quietly, 'but not enough to do anything about it.'

'What was there to do? I mean, there was never any proof of murder.' Dawson stared levelly at Kane. 'Don't misunderstand me, Marshal—none of us cry over a dead Indian, but neither do we kill them. It wasn't so damned long ago when white scalps were hanging in the summer camps of the Sioux and Blackfoot and Crow, and we're not too hasty to forget. But we've kept the peace these last ten years, had some business and pretty well gotten along with them. Yeah, most of the Indians I know are decent people and damned fine hunters, but just like with white folk, there're the bastards among them, too, thieves who plunder other's traps and such like. If one of them gets killed, why I just fold my hands and say a quick "amen" and go on about my business. Nearest sheriff is in Jamestown, ninety miles away, so we're pretty well beholding to our own law up here—which is if you steal, you die. This law has been practical between all hunters, from the Eskimos to the Apache, and we follow that one law and say to hell with the others.'

'A very reasonable law, Mr Dawson,' Kane said, and he meant it. 'But the government is worried about the sharp increase in the Indian death rate, and it'll be my job to find out why. Can I figure on some help from you?'

'Yeah ... if you play it straight and remember what I've been telling you.'

'That I can promise.'

'Okay. And the fellows here will support me if I ask. Right?'

A chorus of assents, grunts, and nods of approval came from the group at the table. Kane, pleased and heartened by the prospect of cooperation, surveyed the crew and then turned back to Dawson. 'Have any strange tracks been seen around these dead Indians?'

'No. By the time we get to them, enough snow has fallen to hide everything.'

'By the sound of it, these deaths are happening to Indians who're pretty much alone. Is that how they live, widely scattered and by themselves?'

'By and large, yes. "Live" might not be the right word; they each have a cottage for the summer, and in the winter they go away. But I understand what you mean, and you're correct. It's the men who live far apart who seem to be the ones dying off.'

Kane nodded and lapsed into contemplative silence. The men lit their pipes, waiting for his next question. The smoke began hanging heavy and gray below the ceiling when at last he spoke again. 'What about border traffic?'

'Hard to say,' Dawson answered. 'It doesn't mean much between here and Canada, and hunters come and go pretty well as they please. There's a fort east of Turtle Mountain, on the Pembina River, and the Canadians patrol the border with a company of soldiers from there, but that's about all. They know most of the American hunters rather well, and seldom care if they cross.'

'Uh-huh. What about strangers? Seen many of them recently?'

'No, at least not hunters. People pass by here as happens most everywhere, but they stick to the trails. What do you think, fellows? Seen any strange tracks while you've been out?'

A couple of men nodded, puffing on their pipes as if collecting their words. Finally one took the stem out of his mouth and ventured: 'Last month I saw tracks of two men and a sled east of Devil's Lake. But it started snowing in the evening, and I lost them.'

The other frowned and talked between clenched teeth, his pipe waving up and down as if in agreement. 'I also saw tracks of a sled and two men. Eight dogs, near as I can reckon.'

Kane leaned forward intently. 'Where?'

'Close to Devil's Lake, a little south of it.'

Kane faced Dawson. 'Were there Indians around there then?'

Dawson's eyebrows lifted. 'Now that you mention it, there were! Snow-Owl and Three-Bear. Isn't that right, Ted?'

The man he addressed blew a smoke ring and said in a bass voice, 'Yup. And Snow-Owl—damn take his mangy skin!—was found as foxbait up there, and Three-Bear—Devil take the scoundrel!—was found on the ice at Devil's Lake, dead as a boiled potato.'

Dawson grinned mirthlessly at Kane. 'See, Snow-Owl and Three-Bear were a mite on the edge of what I was referring to earlier. Seems they had a difficult time differentiating between their traps and somebody else's when nobody was around to notice.'

'They wouldn't have gotten much older if'n I'd had my say,' Ted growled, and cracked his knuckles meaningfully.

Kane asked: 'What about hunters from Canada?'

Tom said hot-headedly: 'If'n you mean do they bother us, the answer is they're a pain in the ass! They travel down from Quebec-ways every damned winter. Most are half-bloods, and not their mothers' best children—if'n they ever knew who their mothers were. Laverne is a choice example.'

'Canadian Indians get this far down, too?' Kane then asked.

'Happens, even if they're afraid to mess with the Sioux. Either the Crows or the Blackfeet must like them as brothers, or else there'd be a fat Indian war on our hands, believe you me.'

'Which tribes are you talking about?'

'Chippewa mostly, along with another Huron group from around Lake Eire.'

'I see.' Kane rolled a new cigarette. He'd just stuck it between his lips and lit a stinker, when the door flew open and banged against the wall. Everybody turned, seeing a man rush in the room, a flurry of snow around him as he brushed his skin peajacket clean. 'Dawson!' he shouted. 'You recall Charlie Bowen?'

'Yeah,' Dawson answered. 'He's that Crow who lives beside Beaver Creek, and calls himself Three Crow.'

The man pulled out a carbine, shaking it excitedly. 'I found him, found him out on the lake! The wolves had been having lunch on him something fierce! This here is his rifle!'

Kane jumped up. 'Which lake?'

'Dawson's Lake, on the other side of the mountain ridge.'

'Don't get ideas, Marshal,' Dawson said heavily. 'It was named after another Dawson. I ain't got that fat a head.'

Ted demanded, 'What in tunket was Charlie Bowen doing that far south, Bill?'

'Don't ask me,' the hunter shrugged, taking off his iced jacket. 'One thing for sure, he was going in this direction. I saw his tracks from Beaver Creek and heading straight for the post. He didn't look to have any supplies along, just his rifle and snowshoes. Probably didn't reach the forest afore the wolves got him.'

'Jesus, and he was a good man,' one of the men murmured.

'For an Indian,' another added.

'For a *man*,' Dawson snapped.

Kane walked over to the newly arrived hunter and asked to see the rifle. Bill handed it over and Kane examined it, a Winchester .44/40, the lock of which was frozen solid. He broke the breech and removed six bullets, one at a time.

'Hmm,' Dawson muttered when he saw the bullets in Kane's hand. 'He didn't shoot at the wolves.'

'He might've frozen to death before they came,' the hunter said, shaking his head. 'Looked to be a big pack, eight or ten of them brutes.'

Kane set the rifle and bullets on the table and looked at Dawson. Dawson blinked back at him, and then caught the same idea buzzing in Kane's mind. 'Lord,' he said quietly. 'The tracks are still out there!'

Kane said: 'I'm going to need supplies.'

'More than that, Marshal; you're going to need a guide, at least at first.' Dawson turned to face the men. 'Who wants to go with him up to Beaver Creek?'

A small lean man got up. Ice blue eyes lit his bearded face. 'I could use a breath of fresh air for Charlie Bowen. He split a meal with me back in seventy-six, when I was on the uppers.'

'Okay, Skinny.' Dawson then said to Kane: 'This here is Skinny MacSween. He might chew your ear off with his gab, but he's one of the best hunters in the territory.'

'Fine by me,' Kane said, nodding to MacSween. 'One more thing—who is Laverne?'

'A French-Canadian,' Dawson answered. 'He's not exactly popular with us, and he's had the law up here after him a time or two. Seems wherever he lights, there's a hard-boiled bunch with him ready for fighting. Until now I never closed the door to any man who needed heat, food, and shelter, but with him it's too much.'

'And the Breed, Charlie?'

'Poison, a hundred per cent bastard. He killed his squaw

by beating her too hard when he was drunk, but nothing could ever be proved. He was thrown out of Fort Turtle across the border, and then linked up with Laverne. Laverne used him to do his dirty work, but for some reason Charlie was scared pissless of Laverne. But hell, that don't matter none any longer. Say hello to your guide, Marshal.'

Kane studied the frail-looking, white-bearded old man.

'Hello, Skinny,' he said dryly.

FOUR

'I can tell by my rheumatism, Marshal,' Skinny MacSween chattered. 'There's going to be some cold weather, some mighty coooold weather! Why, I remember one time along about ten years ago—I think it was about when I picked up this devil in my joints, damn it—it was so cold that the sled wouldn't move. Thirteen dogs and twenty men couldn't budge it, and then us fellers started shooting loose the runners. Made a terrible racket, banging away all the way from Dawson's Lake to the trading post. We were hitting bullets under the runners, that's what lifted the sled, and it was a hell of a lift because I had two hundred skins on that trip. Two hundred and a grizzly, and . . .'

Kane let the torrent of words flow past his ears. He was sitting under a lean-to made of spruce, letting the fire warm his frozen body, and outside he could see the pack of dogs snarling over their half-stiff meat. MacSween had ten dogs; ten shaggy mutts of nondescript breed, though you could notice the mixed blood of wolf, Greenland and Siberian husky. The sled was a long, wide affair made of hickory and willow, with a canvas cover lashed over the provisions—flour, salt, sugar, disinfectant, spring steel for the traps, ammunition, matches, and most everything a hunter would require to last until the start of spring.

They had reached the ridge overlooking Dawson's Lake before dusk, and MacSween had pointed out over the ice-clogged lake to where a black spot was dimly visible. That, he'd said, was the remains of poor Charlie Bowen, God rest his red thieving soul.

MacSween was a talker, just as Dawson had warned, but he was also a doer. He chose a dark nook under the rim of a hillock, around which was a heavy stand of white spruce.

He cleared a small section, using the fallen trees as the foundation of the lean-to, chopping up the branches for the roof and the limbs for fire kindling. The fire was laid close to the rock wall, its crackling heat reflected between the hillock and the lean-to. Above, the moonless sky was clear and star-lit, and the sparks of the fire seemed still more stars as they wafted up through the heavy branches. The warmth melted some of the ice on the rock; Skinny placed a battered black coffee pot under the drip and waited for it to fill with water.

'It's quicker than to melt the snow,' he explained cheerfully. Kane nodded absently, just as he'd been nodding to MacSween's babblings since they left the post, and went out to cut more spruce for their beds. By the time he was done, the coffee was boiling, and then MacSween fried some bacon and beans. They ate while the dogs growled, yapped, and snuffled outside in the snow.

It was good, Kane contemplated; good and peaceful and unspoiled. And if truth be known, he wasn't all *that* cold when they'd set camp, even after the long, grueling trek. The fire was a blessing to a man used to the Southwest, but he'd been able to keep respectably warm along the way thanks to MacSween's hot air and the storm of good clothing heaped upon him at Dawson's. He was dressed in a heavy jacket of wolfskin and pants of fox with the fur turned inside, and a pair of tall moccasins made of hare with the sole of deerskin. The clothing was surprisingly light and pleasant, and the air trapped between them and his woolen underwear kept his body heat in. He'd also been loaned a foxskin sleeping bag, a belt with enough space to fit a long hunting knife and a short, hickory-shaft hatchet, and a Winchester .44/40 carbine. The only weapon he'd brought to Fargo was his revolver, which wasn't much protection against predators and giants like grizzlies. Leaning against one side of the lean-to were his snowshoes, crafted by a Crow working for Dawson, and which had been the cause of much merriment back at the post when first he'd tried to use them. It had taken a few miles of sheer misery before he'd worked the rust out of his ability with them, and by then the post was long out of sight. The laughing, insulting ribaldry had been taken good-naturedly; Kane would've treated these North Country men to the same sort of witticisms if they'd been foolish to venture into his desert territory. It was all part of the game.

But the game was over, and on the morrow the serious work would have to be started in earnest. Kane had in his mind a single goal—to examine minutely Beaver Creek, where the unfortunate Charlie Bowen had lived. Until then, there was nothing to do except enjoy the fire and nod to MacSween's running commentary . . .

'. . . and before I knew it, he was towering over me, largest damned bear I'd ever laid eyes on. Marshal, the dogs backed up, my God, so afraid that they shook themselves inside out until the only thing I could make out was their assholes. The bear was gettin' uglier by the second, shaking the pine tree I was holed in until it done uprooted and clobbered him falling over. I was shooting way to beat all hell, and one plug got him smack in the stomach, *clang* against the axe of the Indian he'd eaten for breakfast that morning, braids, belt, and everything. Then it got really mean, and mashed down a whole mess of trees around him. You could goddamn well see the hole in the forest where the bear was stomping to beat the band, like it was burnt-out ruin, I swear, and where was I . . .? Oh yes, he was roaring and snorting so hard, the splintered axe and the Indian's belt buckle fairly blew out his ass. You know, that when a grizzly gets his dander up, it happens that he often shits on himself, and believe me, Marshal, that's exactly what happened this time . . .'

Kane settled himself comfortably and let Skinny MacSween's blather wash over him like a warming shower. The good taste of the food, spiced with the scent of pine and spruce, mellowed his belly and pleased his nose, and slowly his stiffened muscles relaxed. He let his thoughts concentrate on the following day, figuring that now he could withstand a much longer march. The past four hours had made him shaky in the legs, mostly because of his unaccustomed usage of the snowshoes. But the proper method of using them had returned, and now it shouldn't offer much difficulty to hike with them all day long . . .

'... my last bullet!' MacSween exclaimed breathlessly, waving his mittens. 'So's I pressed off, and don't you think that bullet didn't go zing into his belly where the first one had hit the axe, and it ricocheted up through his chest and right into his brain, damn me if it didn't. It rotated awhile inside his thick skull and then the bear turned crosseyed and fell over, ready for skinning.' MacSween paused, beaming.

Kane cleared his throat. 'Yes. Well——'

'And then when he was nothing but a rug, the dogs were still a-quivering in the same spot with their assholes in the air. So I turned them all inside out and let them suck up some of the bear blood, that was the last time they crept inside themselves at the sight of a grizzly. But, Marshal, I'm sorry to say that this has been pleasant, but I'm mighty tired of a sudden, and so a good-night to you and would you please hold your mouth still long enough for me to fall asleep.'

With that, Skinny MacSween crawled into his sleeping bag and conked out almost immediately.

Kane listened to his guide snoring for a while, then crept into his own bag to think awhile. The fire flickered and grew to embers, and Kane was tempted to get up and restoke it. He didn't feel very sleepy, and was afraid he might stay awake for hours more. He closed his eyes to rest them ... and drifted off into a deep, dreamless slumber.

Kane was pleased to discover next day, that he was not as stiff as he feared he'd be. What little discomfort he felt in his muscles was soon worked out as he traveled behind the sled, waving his arms and shuffling forward on the snowshoes, keeping his legs straight and like pendulums swinging from the hip joints.

'My God,' MacSween said at one point, 'you must've learned the trick before, Marshal. If you get tired, though, you just jump on the sled.'

Kane nodded, but was determined not to take MacSween up on his offer. Before they'd started, Skinny had told him that his winter quarters were quite farther north of Devil's Lake, and Kane was led to understand that this detour to

Beaver Creek would cost MacSween three whole days. Three days of slogging like this! Didn't distances and weather mean anything to these hunters? A three-day trip on horseback in Kane's country was bad enough . . . but in this cold, in the snow, and walking the entire way! Well, if an old-timer with a moniker like 'Skinny' could take it, damned if Kane was going to buckle under, even once!

Late in the afternoon, when the sun was a blood-shot eye on the horizon, they discovered the dead Indian's night-camp—that is, they found the hole in the snow and the fire-melted ice-cake where he'd been.

'Hmm,' MacSween said, tugging at his beard. 'Looks like it didn't go quick for ol' Bowen, or Three Crow, as I guess he liked to call himself. Can you see the mountain ridge over there, boy, the one with the small peak? Behind there is Beaver Creek, and west of the valley is Beaver River where he had his traps. Lots of beaver and fox over that-aways. Maybe I'll take a gander at his traps, seein' as we're in the vicinity. In fact, we might as well stay here for to-night; we'll make it to his cabin by tomorrow night if we do.'

An hour later they were sitting under a freshly built lean-to and enjoying the fire, eating and drinking coffee. MacSween fed the scraps to the dogs while Kane rolled a cigarette, and then MacSween fired up his evil-smelling pipe and sat back to rest everything except his jawbone. Kane interrupted his tall tales only one time, when he asked:

'Skinny, what ever happened to Dawson's face?'

MacSween relit his pipe with a stick from the fire, sucked on it a few times, and then said through the exhaled smoke: 'Well, boy, I's a-tells you. It was many a year ago when Dawson was new to these parts. Came from Missouri, and the few hunters here at that time sure got a laugh out of him, being the sorry specimen he was. Thin as a rail, white as a petticoat, and spitting blood, he was. He was determined to become a hunter, he said, and Old Larson—he owned the post back then—felt sorry for him and gave him a very old muzzleloader and some ratty equipment. A drunken Crow went along with Dawson for half a bottle each day, brandy being cheap in those times, and then the winter closed in and we forgot all about them out there. Now, you gotta remember this was before Little Big Horn and Custer, so the Sioux weren't the kind to mess around with, and as I recall, that particular winter was colder than a well-digger's ass. But damned me, if when the ice melted on the rivers, Dawson didn't come back with a load of fine skins, and said the Crow done drunk himself to death a month before. Old Larson looked at the skins and had to admit there were other hunters who had worse profits that season than Dawson. And that poor relic of a human had put on weight, was brown as hickory, and was rolling in the silver after he sold his skins. Well, the years passed like that, Dawson always showing up with his sled piled high, for it seems the Indian, when sober, had taught him a lot of good tricks before he died, and Dawson had kept his ears clean. Old Larson got to like Dawson, admiring the way he went out there a greenie and showed up the regular hunters, and the way Dawson never drank himself into a stupor but saved his money. Pretty soon Dawson was investing in the post, and when Old Larson kicked the bucket, he left the whole she-bang to Dawson. Dawson had some fancy ideas when he took over. He started the wagons to Fargo, and when the railroad came through, he was all set for the rich buyers alla way from New York. And boy, they had heard of Dawson by this time, these buyers had, for he was one of the few honest ones, who knew good skins and wasn't afraid to pay top dollar for them, but was sharp enough so he never got cheated out of his fair share either.'

This account had rambled slowly between long, turgid puffings on his pipe, which MacSween had to constantly relight. Kane got up and poked the fire awake, adding some fresh kindling, and during one of the frequent pauses, said dryly:

'Skinny, I asked about his face, not his history.'

'I'm coming to that,' MacSween replied, puffing. 'Now, listen. Dawson had a horse, a black mare called "Devil's Mare", and a pretty girl she was, too. He'd taken it as security when another greenhorn had come here to become a hunter. This one was high-class, strictly blueblood, with a long handle like Lindsay Burden-LaCroix, or some such.

He was from Atlanta, and seems he caused a family scandal—got the maid in a family way, so I heard tell at the time—and was forced to go West to make a man outa himself. Seems to me he proved he was a man enough with that maid, but that's aside the point. Well, Dawson gave him his chance, keeping the horse for deposit on the equipment, and just like Dawson had, the boy went out to see what he could see. Only he was too snooty to take an Indian along, drunk or sober, so it wasn't surprising that he was washed up come the spring floods. Seems he tried tangling with a hibernating bear, and unfortunately, the bear woke up. Dawson wrote what had happened to the boy's parents and said he'd send along the horse to them, but after a long while, he got an answer back that if he'd see their son got a Christian burial, he could keep the horse for his trouble.'

'That's nice, Skinny, but what I wanted to know was——'

'You gotta understand, there's Dawson with this here gentleman's horse,' MacSween continued, riding over Kane's objection. 'He felt itchy about keeping it, but when some of his Indians gave him a tip about which bear it was that killed Lindsay Burden-LaCroix, and that the bear was out of its lair for good, Dawson decided to pay it a call. Even things up, you might say. He came back a week later with half his face chewed up.'

'And the bear?'

'You know the skin hanging beside the fireplace? That's it.'

Kane nodded, remembering the enormous pelt and the massive, fang-toothed head.

'It were his Indians who saved him,' MacSween explained. 'They made some kind of goo from roots and tubers and things, and plastered Dawson's mug with it. Stunk like the devil and turned his skin yellow for awhile, but it healed him!'

'That must have been a few years ago.'

'Fifteen.'

'What happened about the horse?'

'Glad you mentioned her, boy, because there's an interesting story about that, too. After Dawson was patched together again, he trained the mare and thought about how to service her. Well, he invited all the stallions around these parts, but the owners would bring them prancing and all hot to trot, and Devil's Mare would turn up her tail and have none of them. News traveled about her, though, and it so happened that the commandant of the Canadian fort on the Pembina heard tell, and it also so happened that he had a thoroughbred stallion with the same problem. Well, down they came to the post, and wham-bang! it took place right on the spot! The commandant barely had time to dismount before his stallion was on her. Well, since then Dawson's gotten three colts out of the deal, and does he love to comb them down when the sun is shining! They're all fine beauties.'

Kane rolled another cigarette while MacSween knocked the dottle from his stinking pipe and refilled it with a gummy looking mixture from a small skin bag. 'How long have you been here?' Kane asked as MacSween lit the new load.

'Since fifty-two.'

'*Fifty-two?*'

'Yes. Shit, how time does fly, eh? I'll be getting onto sixty-four come spring.'

Kane gaped. He'd taken Skinny to be close to fifty, maybe, but hardly any more than that!

'At that time,' MacSween went on, 'we were shooting bear where Fargo is now, and the elk had to go sideways through the woods to not get their antlers stuck.'

'And the Indians?'

'Mostly Sioux, and there were some close occasions when I almost had my hair lifted before we got to know one another. I wasn't careful enough once, and fell for the prettiest little Sioux maid you ever laid eyes on. I ran across her over by Water Lake one summer, and she was sweet as a deer and twice as feisty. I was young and vigorous at that time, and hadn't seen a woman in close to seven years, and things happened pretty much the way they happened between Devil's Mare and the commandant's stallion. She staggered back to her camp sore but happy, and her family raised one hell of a stink. I had to pay them a lot of skins to set things right, and later we all got to be decent friends, and I'd go visiting them during winter with supplies and things. The girl, though, she got married soon after and I never did see eye-to-eye with her brave much. I got to be friends with most of the tribes—Blackfoot and Crow as well as Sioux—and they were almost all splendid fellows in those days. Don't believe what you hear about lyin', thievin' redskins, boy; we whites are the ones who taught them all the tricks. They didn't know what a broken promise was until we did it with our damn fool treaties. There're some really bad ones now, but I can't get too mad at them because I knew a lot of their fathers, who were honorable to the man-jack. I tell you that when the last Indian in Dakota has drunk himself to death, it will leave this country much the poorer. Call me a romantic if you will, but I . . .'

Kane didn't call Skinny MacSween anything, his own estimations of this talkative hunter revising rapidly the longer he was with him. He was forming an unusually high regard for him, and was pleased to know him as a friend. Who else did he know who'd spend a three-day detour in the midst of the trapping season, putting up with an ignorant greenhorn, all because an Indian had shared a meal with him fifteen years before? No, Skinny MacSween was a man to reckon with . . . and man worth riding the river with! He suddenly wished that some of the experience stamped under MacSween's beard was crammed below his own coonskin cap.

'Skinny,' he said, 'I suppose that once you've shown me Beaver Creek, you'll be heading your way?'

'Afraid so, my boy. If we get mild weather, I'll be having to wash and dress my skins.'

'I'll probably be staying in this area for awhile,' Kane said, 'and I sure wish I could know more about it. I've lived south most of my life—along the Rio Grande, from Colorado to the Gulf, and the desert is home for me. This country is new—at least the winters are! Would you teach me about it?'

'My pleasure, boy. I've been a hunter and trapper since I was knee-high to a raccoon, first in the Allegheny Mountains when I was fourteen, and then through most of the northern states and territories, up into Alaska and the Northwest Territory, and even a quick trip to California. No, by God, two times there! Ah, but it's the Northern Lights for me! Now, there's not much time and there's not much I can do for you, but there've been a few things I've picked up which could help you. What do you want to know?'

'Everything,' Kane said.

And MacSween got his foul pipe fuming again and started in to educate the Marshal. The frost creaked in the trees and the lonely wolves howled to a frigid moon, and many times the fire had to be stoked that long, interesting night...

FIVE

'*What the hell!*' MacSween exploded.

Kane pivoted quickly, following with his eyes to where MacSween was pointing. He could see across a small bog, to a small level patch beneath a steep mountain ridge, and in the middle of the clearing were the cold, burnt ruins of a cabin. Sooty beams spread out across the broken, crumbling foundation wall, and a white-frosted chimney stuck upwards in the air like a woolen stump. MacSween and Kane stood staring at the remains, silent with their respective thoughts—and both were thinking the same thing: Here lay the explanation why the Indian calling himself Three Crow was on his way to Dawson's with nothing but a carbine.

'He done burnt himself out,' MacSween said.

'If somebody didn't do it for him,' Kane added quietly.

'Let's have a closer look, boy.'

Grimly, they trudged across the frozen bog, and Skinny ordered the dogs to lay down in the snow. They sniffed and reached their snouts up against the ruins, curious and yet apprehensive.

'Hmm,' MacSween said after awhile. 'Fox tracks. Look there . . . they've been eating Three Crow's dogs.'

Kane studied the bloody bone-stumps and remaining strips of fatty skin and hair. 'They leave a clean table,' he murmured.

'Maybe there're footprints of some two-legged animals about, Marshal. There's Three Crow's tracks there . . . and over there, too. I'll take a trip down to the river and check his traps, and if I'm not back by dusk, you make camp over there by that there dry pine.' MacSween hushed his dogs and began plodding back across the bog, disappearing in-

side the forest.

Kane turned to inspect the burnt cabin. He took off his snowshoes and jumped across the low wall, then hunkered down and started the tedious chore of sifting the ashes. He found a couple of guns—an old Sharps and a still older double-barreled shotgun—their wood burned away and their ironwork fused together. He uncovered the leftovers from the fireplace and a couple of iron cassaroles, but most everything made of metal had melted and were indefinite lumps. He put his snowshoes on again and began circling the ruins ... and it wasn't too long before he discovered tracks.

They were of two men, one of whom had been wearing snowshoes. He bent down to study the impression made by the shoes, but other than the fact their willows were very close, he could make nothing of their pattern. He followed the tracks for some distance and discovered where the other man had removed his snowshoes; there were still the clear, frozen imprints where he'd put them back on and then gone away with the first man. Kane followed their trail up a steep ridge and around in a vague circle along the rim until they ended in an abandoned matting of spruce branches, punctured by deep, hard-frozen identations. At first the indentations confused him, but after thinking about them, Kane laid down and placed his elbows and knees in them and found that they were where the men had lain in the exact same fashion. In this position, he was able to see down along the ridge and between the trees, directly at the cabin.

He got up then and followed the tracks down along the other side. He came to another small bog, grown over with willow, birch, and rowan, and here he discovered the tracks of a sled and a dog team. It was obvious. Here the murderers had parked, going up to watch the cabin awhile and make sure it was empty. Then they'd callously set it on fire and shot the two dogs.

Kane could not hold back the curses he had for these men. It had been a raw, heartless crime, far worse than a mercifully quick bullet through Bowen's—or Three Crow's—brain. He swore mightily, thinking of the dark smudge on the ice and the wolf tracks he'd seen the previous day, and then he set out along the sled trail. It led him through the bog, crossing at the far end, and then sloping up along a gentle pine hill. He reached the top of the hill, but the dark was falling and as much as he wanted to continue, he knew he had to turn back.

The sky was purplish with shadows by the time Kane arrived back at the cabin. He yelled and smote and got the unwilling dogs to their feet, moving them and the sled over to the pine tree MacSween had indicated; it gave good cover, near a ridge where the snow was loose and deep. He had the fire burning brightly by the time MacSween came back, and smiled with a beginner's pride when the grizzled old hunter congratulated him on the job he'd done.

MacSween threw a stiff-frozen fox in the snow, got out his infernal pipe, and grumbled: 'They weren't after his traps.'

'No, they were after Three Crow,' Kane said, and handed MacSween a cup of scalding hot coffee. 'And I've learned something else today—the difference between a hunter and a killer.'

'Eh? How so?'

'Skinny, you're a hunter. If you had an enemy you could burn out, and you came to his cabin when he was gone——'

'I'd never do it!' MacSween snapped. 'I'd face him like a man!'

'Sure you would, Skinny; I'm only saying *if*. Now, there's a lot of skins on the back wall, and being a hunter, you'd not have missed them, right? So if you were going to burn down his cabin, you sure as hell wouldn't leave behind skins worth many hundreds of dollars, would you?'

'God's death!' MacSween burst out. 'I see what you're driving at now, boy. You've got eyes on you, that's for sure.'

'So it strikes me,' Kane continued, 'that whoever burned Three Crow out were professional killers paid for the job, and not hunters or trappers at all.'

'You've got a good head on your shoulders, too. Only way those skins would still be here is if they didn't mean anything to those killers.' MacSween tugged his beard, nodding the stem of his pipe at Kane. 'Boy, you'll do all right out here.'

'No,' Kane said firmly. 'No, I'm not ready yet, and we both know it. But listen, I've found their tracks, and followed them a ways, and it doesn't take much imagination to see how they operated.' Kane related what he'd seen along the ridge and then farther on at the bog, and then angrily, he said: 'Okay, they were hired to burn him out. By whom . . . and why?'

'I don't know who,' MacSween answered. 'But it was to kill Three Crow. Without food or shelter——'

'But listen, Skinny! Three Crow had matches, he had his traps, he even had the warmth of his burning cabin, what was left of it! But he headed straight for Dawson's, and why? Because he was furious, and because he'd seen the same tracks I followed today, and wanted to go after the men but knew he needed fresh supplies to do it. He knew he couldn't by living off his carbine, so he had no other choice but to try for the post.'

'I don't get what you're leading up to,' MacSween said.

'Look at it from the killer's viewpoint, then. They wouldn't know what Three Crow would do when he returned, right? They had no idea where he was; you yourself just said they hadn't checked his traps. If they'd wanted to kill him for sure, they could've hidden themselves up on the mountain ridge and picked him off when Three Crow saw the smoke and came hurrying back.'

'That's an idea,' MacSween agreed. 'But they didn't.'

'They only used that ridge as a look-out spot,' Kane continued. 'Three Crow almost made Dawson's—almost, but not quite! Why did these killers take such a chance? Because they knew it wasn't a chance; because they knew the exact distance to the post from here and figured accordingly?'

'Sure, to make it look like another accident,' MacSween replied. 'But hell, knowing where Dawson's is ain't no big thing. Dawson's is well known throughout the Dakota Territory.'

'Are there any other trading posts around?'

'One, but that's far away, up close to the border and east of the Pembina River. Man from Quebec runs it, and does most of his trading with the Chippewa. What're you thinking about, boy? Come on, spit it out!'

'I think these men burned out Three Crow, but not necessarily to kill him. I don't think they really gave a good God damn whether he lived or died.'

'But why?'

'I've no idea,' Kane admitted ruefully. 'Maybe they wanted his hunting area. No, that's not right. We agreed they weren't hunters.'

'Well, it's damned funny business no matter how it's sliced. Was it just to scare him away?' MacSween mumbled in his beard. 'Frightful way to scare a body out in these parts, I swan.'

'Could be ...'

'Now look at the dinner, Marshal! The meat's burning away to a crisp!' MacSween suddenly jumped up and rescued the skillet from the fire. 'My how you jabber a blue streak, boy. It's downright infectious!'

They ate in silent thought for a long while, and then MacSween looked up from his plate, sniffing loudly. 'Them ruins really stink up the area! I'll come back here in the spring when the ground's soft and see what I can find then. Three Crow had his peculiarities.'

'Did you know him well? I mean, besides that one meal?'

'A little. I think it's the fact we didn't know each other too well that always made that meal stick in my mind.'

'Skinny, draw me a map of the area, will you?'

'Okay.'

MacSween finished the last of his food and set the plate aside. Then, using a flaming branch from the fire, he left the campsite and went off into the woods, returning moments later with a big piece of birchbark. He spit on the bark and spread a paste of crushed charcoal, and using his knife point, drew quickly across the surface. As he made the map, he gave a running commentary.

'We start with Dawson's, northwest of Fargo—here. This is Dawson's Lake where I found Three Crow, and here we are now, Beaver Creek. Beaver River is about here, behind a ridge you can't see from here, and over here is Water River. They run parallel, east to west. And up north is Devil's Lake, and farther north goes Turtle Mountain, with the Canadian fort about ... here. You can see Turtle Mountain from just about anywhere in the area, and so long as it's north of you, you know you're still in Dakota. Now, east of here goes Red River, which runs north and south. In west is Garrison Lake, and then still farther west, out here, is Fort Peck Lake. But then you're in Montana, at the headwater of the Missouri River. Come spring, the snow melts so damned fast in Montana, that Fort Peck Lake swells up and sends excess down to Garrison, which also overflows and spills over into Oahe Lake, the largest reservoir in Dakota. There's a mean one; it's narrow, deep, and it's difficult to say where the river ends and the lake starts. But don't give much thought to that; the point is about the ice loosening in Montana. It's the signal for the ice breaking up on the Cheyenne and Water and Missouri rivers, and that's a danger worth writing home about! Times when whole acres of ice are jammed up on edge, and you can hear the scraping and groaning miles away.'

'When does spring hit these parts?'

'End of March, usually, or the first weeks in April. The winters are bone-cold and dead, but the springs arrive like they're thrown at you. If you should be standing on a river at the end of March and hear it starting to groan under your boot, run for your life!'

'Thanks for the tip,' Kane said. He studied the map after MacSween held the bark over the fire awhile. Now, dried, the birch was brown while the lines were black. Kane folded the bark carefully and slipped it inside his wolfskin jacket, then turned to MacSween and said:

'You're heading home tomorrow morning?'

'Yes. And you? You're staying here like you said you were?'

'I'll be following the tracks,' Kane replied grimly.

MacSween thought about this and then murmured: 'It'll be Satan's own trip, doing it alone.'

'I've no choice, Skinny.'

MacSween tugged his beard, then got up and placed more wood on the fire. One of the dogs stirred, setting the pack to whining; MacSween roared a terrible oath at them and they settled down, meek as lambs. MacSween pestered the fire some more, then came back to sit down beside the Marshal. 'I want to go along with you,' he said at last. 'I get a little fed up with the quiet life, doing nothing but skin, skin, skin.'

Kane smiled tightly, figuring that there was nothing quiet about the existence up here; it was a continual fight for survival, the least relaxation possibly spelling a painful death. 'How .much you estimate you make a week, Skinny?'

'Varies. Fifty dollars, I'd say, if I'm lucky.'

'All right, I'll pay you fifty a week to come along.'

MacSween grinned. 'You think I can help you?'

'I need more than help, Skinny. I need a sled and dogs to carry the supplies; I can't haul it all on my back. Think it over, Skinny. Fifty a week, payable when we get back.'

'Am I going to be a deputy?' MacSween asked carefully.

'Assistant.'

The old trapper's eyes rolled. 'Assistant U.S. Marshal MacSween. Yi! Yi! Does that not sound like a handle and a half! Oath and all?'

'Part of the job, Skinny.'

'Count me in, then! Where are these tracks, anyway?'

'Northeast of here.'

'Why, that's not bad a'tall! That's in the direction of my own cabin, and we might be able to take a look at my skins while we're at it! Eh ... come to think about it, I've been calling you "boy" all this while, and I hope you don't take offense. Just my habit, and hell, I'm old enough to be your dad, Marshal Kane!'

'Call me Morgan,' Kane said, keeping his face sober.

'Dang me! Assistant U.S. Marshal MacSween,' he repeated with veneration. 'Don't that beat all? Well, I'm *your* boy ... Morgan!'

They toasted each other with mugs of boiling coffee.

Gray, soggy-looking clouds scudded overhead when they

started out the next morning, following them while they trailed the sled tracks across the bog and up the pine hill, then down into a dark valley. MacSween swore at his dogs continually, especially when in their eagerness they would drive the sled into rugged ground and become entangled in their harnesses.

'You'd think these mangy critters were the hunters, not us!' MacSween shouted at Kane. 'They've all but beaten their asses off, the way they're running!'

But despite the fearful pace and the old trapper's constant involvement with his team, MacSween still found odd moments to teach Kane the lay of the land. In the middle of a curse he was apt to say: 'Look there—the track of a deer! Poor thing is worn to the nubbin in this loose snow. Why, I've seen deer standing frozen stiff in four feet of snow during really bad winters.'

Or he might call out: 'There, those round points. Mountain lion, and he's sure on the hungry prowl! They don't have it fat during this season, and—hey! A couple of rabbits, and they're up'n running; must be a fox close by . . .'

The hours passed. The trail of Three Crow's killers swung between a row of steep, snaggle-toothed boulders, and several times Kane and MacSween had to loosen the dogs when they tangled their lines in the scrub. 'Chre-rist! Good for nothing but wolf bait!' he'd yell at the dogs then, swinging his axe wrathfully.

They camped in a pocket gorge with a huge spruce forest surrounding them. The dogs discovered a deep snowdrift and dug themselves in, and MacSween, mollified with a meal in his belly, talked on about his animals.

'We only use dogs as draught animals during the winter. At first we tried horses when there was a crust of snow, but they'd cut their hooves and sink through half the time, and often we'd end up having to shoot them. The Crows were the ones who gave us the notion of dogs—their villages are littered with them in the winter, and they rig loads on them to give their squaws a break. We found out how they make sleds in Alaska and that worked out fine, and in loose snow, there's nothing like eight–ten dogs to pull you through. But we stick to horses in summertime; did you see their winter stables at Dawson's?'

Kane nodded.

'Tomorrow night, you'll have to make camp alone, Morgan,' MacSween went on with a sudden change of subject. 'I'm going to head for my cabin—it isn't very far—but you'll have the sled and dogs. Wait in the camp until I return ...'

Next evening, Kane did as MacSween had instructed, remembering how MacSween had fashioned the lean-to and fed the dogs strips of stone-hard meat. It was colder than it'd been before, and Kane snuggled into his sleeping bag, drinking boiling coffee while waiting for his own dinner to cook. The sparks flickered up between the spruce branches overhead, and in a space between the dark tree crowns he could see a glimpse of the ice-blue new moon...

He was still having a hard time with the knowledge that he was on more than a simple hunting trip in the wilderness. He'd seen the cabin ruins and the remains of the dogs; seen Three Crow's presence in the dark spot on the ice—but it somehow remained impersonal to him, so far from the violence and death to which he could relate: the sudden shots, the stalking in gloomy cantinas west of Pecos, the dusty horses, the dried-up waterholes ... Change took awhile for Morgan Kane, and now it was as if he sensed his real enemy this far north was the north itself, with its cold, barren, snow-whipped vastness.

Even at the moment, knowing he was alone, he had the strange feeling he was being watched. That somebody or something was out there beyond the fire, staring ... waiting ... Kane forced himself to remain rigid in the sleeping bag, though his nerves screamed for him to jump up and run. His eyes drifted to the Winchester sheathed in its case nearby, and the heaviness of his Colt revolver pressed against his stomach inside the bag. It was his imagination working overtime, it had to be ... but no, now the dogs had ceased their growling ...

Kane's nerves were ready to burst. He lifted his hands and blew on them, then stuffed them inside his jacket opening, easing out the revolver while shaking himself closer to the dark wall. He propped himself up on his left side, fingers curling around the gun butt, his thumb gently caressing the knurled hammer, perspiration beginning to trickle down his temples despite the bitter temperature.

One of the dogs suddenly barked, as if in warning. Kane took his left hand out of the bag and tossed a large branch on the fire; the flames shot up, but he saw no one. He cocked the hammer, the small sound muffled under the jacket and bag ... Then he heard another sound, the sound of softly padding feet approaching from the shadows. He wasn't wrong! Somebody was out there!

He turned his head slowly in the direction of the noise, and from the darkness there appeared a tall, bent shape dressed in skins, long greasy hair hanging down below the edge of his cap.

An Indian!

The Indian had the dead body of a marten in his left hand, and clutched in his right was a long-barreled rifle. Kane noticed the hammer was pulled back on the rifle, ready to fire at an instant's notice, even though the butt rested against the Indian's thigh and the muzzle was pointed between the fire and Kane himself.

'I am Grey-Wolf,' the Indian said, and his deeply solemn voice jarred Kane, made the sweat come freely to his forehead.

'Welcome,' Kane managed. 'Are you hungry?' He didn't move, but under his jacket he pointed the revolver at the Indian. 'I have food, if that is what you want.'

'I want whiskey,' the Indian replied.

'No, no whiskey,' Kane said, shaking his head. 'Only coffee.'

'Whiskey!' Grey-Wolf repeated harshly, and shook the marten pelt at Kane. 'I come with this, worth twenty dollar! Worth much whiskey!'

Kane shook his head more firmly. 'I don't have any whiskey.'

The Indian's black eyes flashed against the fire. 'White man always have much whiskey. I know. Take marten, much worth!' He threw the pelt in front of Kane's bag. The beautiful rich fur gleamed in the firelight. 'Now, whiskey! I have given you marten ... you give me my whiskey!'

The dogs were barking regularly now, and a sprig of wood snapped short and sharp in the fire, fraying Kane's nerves still further. Still he forced himself to remain where he was with a mask of calmness hiding his emotions. An incidental thought occurred: would he burn the skin off his chest if he had to shoot?

'No whiskey,' he repeated stubbornly, and nodded toward the sled. 'Take a look for yourself, Grey-Wolf.'

The Indian never moved. 'You lie!' he snapped, and Kane could see the brutish anger welling in the redman's eyes. 'You lie, all whites lie! I know you have whiskey!'

Grey-Wolf whipped the muzzle up and toward Kane, snarling as he aimed at the bag and the prone man lying in it. Kane shot, the blasting shot ripping through the forest quiet from beneath his jacket. The Indian staggered backwards, dropping his rifle and clutching his chest, and with a rattling groan he fell over in the snow, just outside the gleam of the fire.

Kane tore from the sleeping bag, revolver ready for another shot. A burnt, sour smell came from the lining of his jacket, and pain seared along his flame-scarred ribs. He moved quickly to where the Indian sprawled, grasping him by his feet and dragging him into the light again. Snow frosted the Indian's bushy brows, melting now and running down into his eyes and beyond, over his cheeks as if he were crying. Kane stared down at the tears of death, breathing hard, wishing desperately that he had the booze the Indian had demanded. He fingered the dark-rimmed hole in his jacket and the red burning welt along his side; tomorrow he'd have to sew up the hole and bandage the blister. In the meantime . . .

He grasped the Indian by his feet again and pulled him out into the darkness, covering him in a mound of snow. Then Kane sat down on the foxskin bag and rolled a cigarette with shaking fingers. He inhaled the pleasant smoke. The Indian's rifle, his own carbine and revolver were all handy and in good repair; he wondered why he didn't feel safe, and thought of a thousand questions to ask the dead Indian:

Had Grey-Wolf come on foot? Had he a sled, and if so,

was the sled still nearby? How had he discovered the camp? Had he followed tracks, or seen a reflection of the campfire? No, not the last, not in this narrow valley! He must have been following the tracks for quite some time, and waited until MacSween had left ... one against one were proper odds. But why had he brought along the marten? To do business as he'd professed? Did white hunters usually bring whiskey along in such large amounts they could bargain for pelts with it? *I know* the Indian had said, but what had he known . . .?

The answer seemed close, right on the tip of Kane's mental tongue, and Kane sat by the fire for most of the night, trying to pull the answer from his subconscious. He couldn't seem to clutch it, no matter how he struggled with himself. And the dogs continued barking out in the darkness, scenting the heady fragrance of freshly spilled blood.

SIX

'Grey-Wolf, all right,' MacSween said, brushing the snow from the frozen, dirty face. 'A Crow, always hanging around Dawson's bumming whiskey until he was thrown out. His people chased him out of their camps, too. Real sonofabitch, and thank God you managed to plug him instead of the other way around. Last time I'll laugh at that pea-shooter of yours, Morgan, but damned if that wasn't a lucky shot, right through your jacket!'

Kane looked away from the Indian he'd killed. 'What are we going to do with him?'

MacSween spit in the snow. 'Let him stay here.'

While breaking camp, MacSween told Kane of his trip to his cabin, and how he'd prepared his skins and hung them up to dry. 'Didn't see any strange tracks,' he concluded, 'Though God help any bastard foolish enough to mess with my stuff!'

The rest of that day they followed the now week-old tracks northward, Kane growing increasingly competent with his snowshoes and the handling of the dogs. He'd learned the commands to get them running or stop them in their tracks, and grew familiar with how to operate the harness and pick the best track for the sled. They began to exchange places, MacSween allowing Kane to drive under his guidance, and along about nightfall, the old trapper said:

'We're picking up speed this way. Must be closing in on them at this rate. You're a fast learner, Morgan!'

They camped again, ate and bedded down, and woke to a morning filled with barking and fighting between the dogs. The gray light of dawn grew brilliant as the new day progressed, and in the afternoon, MacSween drew to a halt along the crest of a mountain ridge which was black and naked after a previous year's forest fire.

'This is Four Hill,' MacSween explained.

Kane blew his nose against his mitten and glanced around. As blighted as the burnt trees appeared, the view from the hill was spectacular. Below wound the dark band of the Cheyenne River, and once Kane had been told this, he could easily orient himself by remembering the birch-bark map. Eastward was the broad oval of Dawson's Lake, and northward were the Cheyenne and Water lakes from which frozen rivers mouthed. Farther north rose Turtle Mountain, far off and sharp with a sparkle of blue from the ice surrounding its peak. To the west were a series of ridges, sawtoothed with pointed cones and deep valley gaps, and Kane could just catch the glimmer of Garrison Lake beyond, the reservoir of the Missouri River.

MacSween peered intently, squinted because of the shining reflection of ice and snow. 'They're someplace down in the valley. My bones tell me so.' His forehead wrinkled beneath his shaggy hair. 'Now, Beaver Creek forks not far from here, and the east branch runs close up by Deer Skull Creek and then easterly, toward Aberdeen and south of Fargo. Where the creek runs through this valley, there should be a Crow camp around someplace. Can you see any smoke, Morgan?'

Kane shielded his eyes to the glare, and very faintly, he thought he could see the wisp of tell-tale gray smoke against the green of the trees and the blue-white of the sky. 'Is that it?' he asked, pointing.

'Yeah, I think so,' MacSween confirmed. 'You see damned well, Morgan. My eyes ain't what they used to be, damnit.'

'If I saw it, you can bet those two killers have as well,' Kane commented dryly. 'I wonder if they split to the north or the south of the camp?'

'Best way to find out is follow their trail down the ridge and see how they duck,' MacSween replied, and lashed the dogs into action. They slid down the slope and through the valley a short ways, and then MacSween reined in the dogs again. He scratched his head and tugged his beard.

'Damned if they aren't heading straight for the Crows,' he said. 'Well, I guess that means we are too!'

Kane didn't respond, but felt a clamminess settled between his shoulder blades. The forest was thick in the valley, and they had a hard job pulling the sled through before they reached the frozen creek and could follow it downstream toward the camp.

Then, suddenly, there came a distant rifle shot ringing across the still land. 'Yi!' MacSween shouted. 'Let's go!' They thrust themselves against the sled, taking it across the snow as fast as they dared, the dogs racing with tongues panting in an effort to keep ahead. The two men staggered and stumbled through the forest, and now more shots crackled, becoming louder.

Now they were deep in the valley spruce, away from the creek and in the direction of the rifle shots, and MacSween paused long enough to dig his rifle from its sheath. Kane fingered his carbine and the revolver inside his jacket. Then, leaving the sled, they returned to the creek and moved quickly and quietly along its bank. A sharp scream splintered the air.

'Crow!' MacSween hissed. 'Watch out, their camp should be right over there!'

A gust of sulphurous smoke drifted between the spruce, and the high-pitched scream came again, a wail of pain now. Kane suddenly spotted something moving between the trees, and grasped MacSween's arm, forcing the hunter down into a crouch.

He whispered: 'A man!'

'Indian?'

'No.'

'Shoot him, then!'

They split up, Kane creeping behind a thick tree trunk. He spied the shadowed figure again and bent down with his carbine in hand. He aimed carefully and squeezed the trigger.

The figure gasped, whirled around and disappeared in the snow. 'Somebody's coming!' His cry resounded heavily through the wood.

'Laverne!' MacSween growled. 'I'd know his voice anywhere.'

Kane took a firm grip on the carbine and crept to a knoll. He glanced back at MacSween, seeing the snow puff up around the old hunter as he jumped up and threw himself behind a stump. More shots peppered around Kane's guide, and angrily, Kane answered with a couple of quick bullets. The man who'd been with Laverne and had been firing at MacSween fell over in the snow, his snowshoes sticking straight up in the air.

'A Chippewa,' MacSween said, low and breathless. 'Laverne must have brought some along with him against the Crow. They hate the sight of one another, y'know, and unless I miss my mark, they won't have left much of that village standing by now!'

'We've got to split up, Skinny,' Kane said, searching the dark woods around them. 'We stay here together, and they'll surround us in no time.'

'You're right. Good luck, boy!'

Kane moved cautiously with his rifle held ready, heading toward that wisp of smoke. He paused, hunching down to reload ... and then suddenly heard the creak of snowshoes nearby. He pivoted around and saw a grimacing Indian raising his rifle. His own carbine was still broke open; Kane grappled for his revolver and two shots rang out at the same time. He saw the flame belching from the Chippewa's rifle and felt a lead bullet tug at his hat—but he also had the pleasure of seeing the Chippewa's face explode in a reddish smear, the hate-filled grin wiped off as the body fell over.

Kane instantly circled behind another stump and glanced out over the late afternoon shadows. It would be dark soon, a very bad time to be caught alone. Some distance away, dogs were giving tongue, and then abruptly there was another shower of bullets. Flames leaped at him from the brushwood, and in desperation, Kane levered and shot as fast as he could, directly at the rifle fire. He heard a gurgle, and knew he'd hit one of them at least. He bent down and reloaded again, dropping a couple of bullets in his haste; beads of perspiration rivuleted down his cheeks, and he was soaking wet beneath his jacket.

Where were they? And how many ...?

Slowly he began to sneak along the snow-covered scrub, seeing in the dim light many footprints. No sign of the bushwhackers themselves, though. Had they fled? Tendrils of smoke curled through the trees, stinging his nostrils and making his eyes water with its sour, gray odor. He wiped away the water and crawled forward ...

Clang!

A sharp punch was thrown against his rifle and it was nearly torn from his grip. He threw himself flat and got out the revolver again, unsure how badly the carbine was damaged by the bullet meant for him. He spotted movement between the trees; a heavily dressed figure with its rifle leveled. Kane rolled himself to one side while a shot buzzed past his ear like a maddened wasp. Then he raised up and shot three times in quick succession, seeing bark chips flying from the tree trunks. A man jerked forward, fell to his knees, and began to shuffle for cover. Mercilessly, Kane sighted on the man and smashed his spine with a single shot. Kane dropped, waited for more ...

Silence once more blanketed the forest.

Then: 'Morgan ...?'

'Skinny?'

'Yeah. I'm over here.'

Carefully Kane rose up. MacSween was squatting on his knees beside the dead man. 'One of Laverne's,' he said. 'I heard the rest of them vamoosing; they already had dogs and sled set to move out. We've got to take a look at that Crow camp—and I tell you, I feel that we'll find a slaughter!'

Together they edged toward the camp, wary of every shadow and sound. They reached the Indian settlement safely, though, and entered a small clearing where once five cabins had been standing. The embers were still smoking, nothing of the cabins remaining upright, the surrounding snow melted like moss and autumn-brown grass showing through the gray and black ash. They removed their snowshoes and went slowly around the camp, shaking their heads with horror.

'God almighty,' MacSween whispered. 'Look at this!'

Four dead dogs were lying in the rubble. The body of an elderly man sprawled with his head in the embers, his legs spread out in the wilted grass. There were two bullet holes in his back. A short distance away were two women, one old and one very young, but both were so badly burnt it was impossible to tell if they'd been shot or not. A little child was curled by the edge of the clearing, no hair on her head and a small wooden doll clutched hopelessly in one charred hand.

Kane felt close to being sick. He turned away and stumbled from the stinking graveyard and leaned against a tree, the world going around before his eyes. *Why here?* cried out in his mind. *Why here ... inside this wood ...?* It was completely without meaning! To wipe out an entire camp of poverty-stricken Indians ... to ruthlessly murder the old, the sick, women, and children ...

MacSween walked up beside him, his face bleached beneath his beard. 'Bastards,' he said, flustered and shaking. 'This is the worst thing I have ever laid eyes on in my life, bar none!'

Kane rubbed a shaking hand across his lips. 'We have to do something about them. We can't just leave them like this.'

'They were Christians,' MacSween said softly. 'The ground is soft, thanks to the fire. We can bury them, at least.'

They got out their shovels and after awhile, they got out the double-bladed axe that was packed on the sled. The frost on top had melted, but farther down the ground was as stone. They fashioned a crude common grave and gently laid the dead villagers into it, and Kane filled it back in while MacSween lashed together two sticks to form a primitive cross.

Dark as it was by the time they finished, they drove the sled far from the massacred clearing, where the air was clean and there were no smells to excite the dogs or remind them of what they'd seen.

'Tomorrow,' MacSween promised fervently when the camp had been made. 'Tomorrow we circle the valley and find the tracks. Wouldn't surprise me none if these killers don't meet on the other side and head on as a bunch. Clean that pocket gun of yours, boy, and I'm going to grind my knife to a razor edge. I haven't taken a scalp in twenty years, but by God if'n I catch one of those murderin' heathens, I'm going to lift me a hank of hair, and while he's still living.'

A little later, MacSween said: 'You notice there were no men in that village, Morgan?'

'Yes. They were all out hunting?'

MacSween nodded. 'Probably up around Garrison Lake. Not more than five or six of them, but I sure wish they were with us now. When they *do* get back ... yi!'

MacSween proved correct in his prediction. Next day they discovered a mingling of tracks, and sorting them out, there seemed to have been four men from Beaver Creek and six from Dawson's Lake joining together east of the burnt-out camp. Their direction was unmistakable—north, toward the Pembina River.

'Heading for the border, eh?'

Kane was answered: 'I'd say so, Morgan.'

'Think it might be a trap?'

MacSween thought for a moment, then said: 'No, I doubt it.'

They started following the tracks. MacSween said as they traveled: 'Laverne must've had his Chippewas close by when he left Dawson's post. They linked up with Three Crow's killers when they massacred the village. M'God, have they gone crazy?'

Kane shook his head wearily. All murder was crazy, but there's usually some rationale behind it. It bothered him greatly that he couldn't figure out what the reason behind this blood-letting was this time. 'How long will it take us to reach the Pembina?'

'Two, maybe three days. Depends on the weather. We better lay out some traps and spend the morning catching some meat, at least for the dogs. I'll rig up some rabbit snares with the wire I've got along—used to be lots of rabbits out on the levels ...'

When once again the day darkened into night, MacSween

headed for some deep woods about three miles from a tall, prominant ridge. 'They could be camping in the other side,' he said sourly. 'The thought of them Crow braves coming back might've added wings to their feet!' Kane smiled darkly at the thought.

While they were cutting kindling for the fire, MacSween paused and sniffed the air, a worried expression growing on his face. 'It's warming up. That means we're in for snow, Morgan. Damn! I sure hope we're not in for a full-sized blizzard.'

Kane stared northward, toward the black ridge. *Not now*, he inwardly begged. *Please not now* ... But during the night he awoke to the stirring of the trees and the groaning of ice. During the morning, the first snow began falling through the tree crowns, and then the wind became stronger, forcing the snow into drifts and packing the flakes against the sled. Kane would brush himself and the powdery white snow would fly about his ears.

'No storm yet,' MacSween told him. 'We've got to hurry before the snow covers their tracks!'

There was a quick breakfast, and while Kane broke camp, MacSween checked the traps. The old trapper came back with some rabbits which he threw on the sled, and then they were off, urgency dogging their heels. Across the bog they hurried, the wind growing until it was almost blinding them with its howling fury. Snow stuck fast to Kane's jacket, and the ridge ahead was no longer black but a pale ivory crest blending with the low country.

MacSween urged his team on, the sled sliding across the new snow pack without the usual sound of creaking ice beneath the runners. They reached the shelter of the ridge, the tracks of the hunted killers long since dissipated, but still they kept on, swearing and cursing the dogs until they topped the rocky peak. Kane fought his way through the deepening snow, finding it like frigid quicksand, neither sticky—it was still too cold for that—nor especially loose, either. It seemed to drag him down, no matter what he tried, and pausing momentarily on the summit, MacSween turned around to him and grinned: 'This is only a foretaste of things to come, Morgan. But we'll soon make camp so you can lay down and rest in your beddy-poo.'

Kane swore at him, having to admit privately that Skinny could drive him near distraction. He promised that if he could ever lure the old fossil south, he'd show him a few obnoxious tricks in return!

But MacSween only laughed, tickled that he'd gotten the Marshal's goat, and then turned serious. 'Strange,' he noted. 'This is normal for autumn when the storms come. I hope to God we're not in for a blow now.'

His words were useless; it became increasingly thicker, the snow in flurries so dense it was hard to see through them. Turtle Mountain glimmered in the nearby distance, the massive top of ice twinkling through the shower of snow. MacSween pointed to the northeast of it, commenting: 'Pembina River is in this direction, and we should be there by tomorrow—I hope! If the weather worsens, we'll have to hole up and pray it doesn't last over four days. But I know the area pretty well, so you don't have to quake in your boots as if we were in Alaska!'

This time Kane laughed with the old trapper, even though it was a forced laugh, for he was truly very concerned. This was all so new to him ... too new for comfort. He spied through the snow the expanse of a wide valley of pinewood and naked rock toward the west of them. The valley seemed endless as it sloped down from the ridge where they stood; it would be easier going from here on in, at least, and not so bad going up the other side...

Kane was wrong.

Half-way up the opposite side of the valley, he learned how dearly the sled wished to turn over in the loose-packed snow. They and the dogs struggled and rolled in the deep drifts, and the sled was roundly cursed by both MacSween and Kane, though it didn't seem to have any effect on it. They ended up having to zig-zag in a switch-back trail to reach the summit, and then once again perched on top of a ridge, MacSween told Kane: 'Take what'll probably be your only look at the Cheyenne River, Morgan,' and Kane panted in response that it was all he cared to see.

The snow was not as deep on the rim because of the wind, but that only meant more of it was flying in their faces. Kane got only ellusive glimpses of the high elevations stretching northward, and the silhouettes of high mountain plateaus he'd have called buttes.

'Bison country,' MacSween said. 'There're piles of their bones in the peat there, left over after the hunters cleaned the area starting some thirty years ago.'

'Tough for the bison,' Kane said laconically. He was too done in to weep over the dead animals, longing for nothing more than camp, food, warmth, and rest. Yeah, and beddy-poo...

MacSween roared at his team and they continued on at a fast trot toward the next ridge, and the wind was hard and solid against them. The snow was like a smoking, storming ocean, dead cold and thundering, whistling down from the border mountain and breaking over the tall stands of timber. It was dusk when they reached the protection of the next ridge, and here MacSween stopped to moan:

'It was close, Morgan, I have to admit it!'

He gripped his axe and stumbled away from the sled, and shortly afterward he and Kane were erecting a breaker-wall of spruce and pine. It was far more than a lean-to this time; it was a veritable screen with the tarpaulin of the sled stretched over it as a roof, and the sturdy branches plugged with smaller limbs until they had a miniature cabin able to last until spring if necessary. And outside the storm heaved and thundered against them, and higher up on the ridge they could occasionally hear a mighty tree cracking and falling under the weight of the driven snow.

The fire crackled clear and high and the freshly caught rabbits were dressed, fried in bacon grease, and hung away while MacSween and Kane ate the rest of the dried deer meat. It took a lot of grease before the deer began to resemble something edible, and Kane stared at the dripping rabbits with an obvious desire.

'The hell with you!' MacSween laughed. 'I've plenty of wire; we'll have more rabbits than you'll care to eat!' And with that he took one down to share for dessert.

Kane took care not to give a long and unpolite belch afterward, even though it was a sign of his contentment. He felt close to throwing his marshal's star away and forgetting

Shane, forgetting Leavenworth, forgetting his mission here in Dakota. He lay back listening to the groaning of the forest, smelling the crisp clean odors of the spruce and watching the leaping tendrils of the fire—and a warmth spread through his tired body, a sweet aching in his overworked muscles pleasant and full of satisfaction. But as he continued to stare at the flickering flames, he seemed to see Grey-Wolf's black maddened eyes in them, and could hear the echo: *Whiskey for the marten ... I know you have whiskey, white man* ... And he recalled the burnt village of the Crows and the wooden doll clutched in the massacred girl's hands, and the old man naked with black frozen feet ... and the good feelings iced out of him. No ... he could not forget his reason for being here, he concluded. Death was his twin, and death showed clearly in the tracks of the killers, and Three Crow's dark blot on the ice ... and the Dakota Territory with its Cheyenne River and howling storms became only a memory to him of every other mission he'd had to pursue. He could no more escape his destiny than he could allow Laverne and his murderous gang to escape theirs ...

MacSween stared silently down into his coffee cup, and Kane wondered if the grizzled veteran of these hills was seeking a personal answer too. And then he turned away, leaving his friend to his short spell of privacy, and heard the storm drone and growl through the trees, the snow falling in droves, and once again he contemplated the awful sight he'd witnessed at the Crow camp. He hoped that the snow would hide the burnt-out wreckage until spring, and then the new season would cover the blight with flowers and green, promising grass.

SEVEN

The morning arrived gray and seething. The wind blew around the camp, and the dogs struggled to their feet, shaking themselves and sending showers of snow in every direction. It was colder, but still it was snowing.

'Come on,' MacSween ordered. 'We're leaving. I think the worst of the storm is over enough to risk it.'

Within a half an hour they'd packed the sled and harnessed the dogs and were driving away from their shelter. Kane noticed that the cloud cover was not as low as it'd been the previous day, but the wind was sharper, forcing him to keep his head down. Tears rolled from his eyes and froze along his cheeks, and he continually rubbed his face and nose to renew the circulation, MacSween warning him that the wind was a greater danger than the cold itself.

The dogs leaned into their traces until the harness was strained and singing. Snow whirled around them all, rising into wave-like crests from which the wind blew crusted ice as if it were ocean spume. The mountain ridge for which they headed seemed impossibly distant and unapproachable. Kane tried to judge how far it was, but the snow was like white smoke, blurring what little he could see through slitted eyes. It was all he could do to keep pace with the sled and the swaying, icy back of MacSween ahead of him.

Slowly the ridge grew closer, and eventually Kane could make out a few details, and the crooked spruce on its top which was lying nearly flat from the combined weight of the wind and snow. They reached a small cove, and for a moment the violent northern wind was silent and gone, and Kane was able to catch his breath and break some of the accumulated ice which hung on his clothing. The dogs were totally white, with frozen caps on their rough fur and down around their legs. MacSween gestured up toward the mountain ridge, Kane nodding in exhausted agreement, and once again they urged the sled forward.

Then suddenly MacSween stopped and bent down. Kane rushed to him, afraid for the old trapper's health, but beneath the ice-crusted beard he saw a broad, healthy grin. There, at MacSween's feet, was the very faint outline of a sled.

MacSween straightened, his red-rimmed eyes sparkling and he pointed to the woods with one hand and held a mitten over his lower face with the other. It was even too cold for talking, but Kane understood immediately. The track could not be many hours old or it would have been completely snowed over. What luck that the trees had protected this spot, and they'd discovered it!

But it was not entirely due to luck. Assuming MacSween was right about the raiders heading toward Pembina River, then it was logical they'd go the same way as he and Kane, for it was the shortest and safest route. But then came another thought to Kane: both parties must have spent the night in the same woods, probably one on each side—and the notion of having been so close to his quarry galled the Marshal and sent the blood pounding through his chest.

They moved on with renewed determination. MacSween directed the sled carefully through the trees, and here and there they were able to detect other tracks. They all pointed up the slope to the ridge, sleds one after another and men on snowshoes beside them, their trail only faint strips at the best of times underneath the sheltering trees, and completely wiped away by the wind when crossing an open patch.

Kane moved close to MacSween and shouted in his ear: 'You think they're going to camp on the ridge?'

MacSween nodded. 'Probably on the other side,' he yelled. 'It'll be getting dark in a couple of hours; we'll leave the sled below the summit and walk over.' His voice was hard as flint, the voice of a hunter stalking the kill.

Kane bustled upward, breaking the sled loose once when it got stuck, straightening the harness, and throwing a snarling dog back into its place in line. Finally the ridge flattened out, and MacSween dragged the dogs toward a ledge and got them to lie down beneath it, in its cover. Then he and Kane broke limbs from the neighboring trees and placed them over the sled to stop the snow from packing. They checked their rifles, working the movements to free the oil and making sure they were loaded with bullets, and then taking handfuls of extra ammunition, they began the hike across the top of the ridge and down along the other side.

'One bit of luck,' MacSween said in a low voice. 'The wind is against us so we'll be able to smell their fire.'

The wind shifted a little, but still it hit them in the face, and now the snow was turning into pellets of hail which stuck to their faces and burned their skin. Kane followed MacSween closely, moving his arms and walking with pendulum strides. The thought of being outnumbered by merciless killers didn't bother him; his nerves were screaming for release after the hard days and the terrible memory of the massacred Crows.

Twilight lengthened with the shadows of the valley, and the roar of the wind through the treetops seemed somehow far away and unreal. Then the smell of smoke flared his nostrils, and by the way MacSween's back stiffened, he could tell his friend had noticed it too. They headed slowly in its direction through the spruce, among the snow-covered stumps and underbrush, keeping the wind in their faces. They came very close to a tall, steep bluff which was dark below its overhang, and MacSween crouched, Kane creeping up beside him. The smell of the fire was thick now.

'I think they've made camp under the overhang, Morgan,' MacSween whispered. 'Think you could climb it?'

Kane nodded.

'I'll move up in front of them, and when you're shooting down, boy, be sure you don't aim at me! I don't think their dogs will notice you up there, even though the wind will be in your back.'

Kane looked sharply at the old trapper, wondering if he were being sent up the bluff to keep him out of harm's way. Kane didn't like it if that were true; he didn't like it in any case, for MacSween was placing himself in a very dangerous position, sneaking close where the ground was level. But the Marshal also realized it would be useless to argue, MacSween being as obstinate as the grizzly bears he hunted.

MacSween took off his mitten in reckless disregard for the weather, and stuck his hand out to Kane. 'Good luck, boy. Be sure to wait for me!'

Kane squeezed the cold fingers, then turned and began his ascent up the steep overhang, taking a curving path around to conceal his presence. The wind whipped mournfully across the ridge, but Kane noticed only his hate-filled heart beating, taking care to protect his carbine from the snow and hail. Every moment he expected to hear a sharp report behind him, but it never came ... the wind sighed and grumbled and the trees scraped their heavily laden branches against his thick jacket. The overhang was no longer above him now, but directly to his right, and he moved toward it carefully, wondering if he should remove his snowshoes. His common sense told him he'd be quieter going through the thicket if he did take them off, but if he did, he must keep them with him in case he had to make a quick escape. He unstrapped them, then buckled them together and threw them over his shoulder.

He sunk into soft snow up to his knees, but in the scrub, he found he actually made better time with the snowshoes off. Then he came to the overhang itself, and found himself looking down some thirty yards to the valley below. He slowly crept forward across the plateau, the sweat running beneath his jacket and his hair plastered to his scalp beneath his cap. He saw a flicking, ghostly-looking light fluttering over the top of the spruce below him, and realized it was the reflection of the fire blazing beneath the overhang. He crawled closer, the glimmering flames growing clearer and the wind whining upward in the draft, and then he was at the rim of the overhang and able to see directly down into the raider's camp below.

The site had been well chosen in a vee between two smaller overhangs, and sleds were parked on either side. There were the sounds of knives scraping plates and the clink of cups against the large pot as coffee was poured, and the constant murmur of voices which drifted up along with the wind. And Kane stared down at the vividly contrasting sight of the camp against the black impenetrable woods and thought of that crazy hunter, Skinny, sneaking up on them alone.

He searched the surrounding dark spruce with his eyes, but didn't see a sign of MacSween. Only the sleds, looking similar to their own, heavily loaded and covered with tarps. Not even the dogs were in the circle of firelight, and possibly they'd dug themselves in for the night. He spotted at least four guns resting near the sleds, and none of the half-dozen men seemed to have weapons within easy reach; obviously they felt smugly secure. The men were dressed in skin, and two of them had something which resembled anoraks with hoods snugged tightly over their heads. The smell of mutton reminded him how hungry and thirsty he was, but the view of those killers thirty yards away overwhelmed him with impatience.

Where was that blasted MacSween?

Kane shifted positions, moving to a better position from which to aim the Winchester. He levered the first bullet into the chamber, lying flat on the snow with his elbows bent and the carbine sighted, and his finger itched on the trigger.

Wait for me, MacSween had said . . .

The snow lay grayish-white against the dark trees. Kane gripped and regripped his carbine, feeling his hands growing numb with cold. He put his mittens back on and wriggled his fingers back and forth, and did this several times while the endless minutes of waiting passed. Then, abruptly, a shot sang out, echoing up to him, followed by another one almost immediately. He saw the quick flash from MacSween's gun from a tangled scrub of spruce, and then he sent off four bullets as fast as he could.

Two of the men below fell flat on their faces, while two others leaped desperately for the fire. Kane knew at once what they had in mind—to douse the flames! He shot twice more, and MacSween felled one of the men at the fire, sending him sprawling into the flames. The fire burst up around the man's jacket, then began to die; in the remaining flickers, answering bullets began to whip up around Kane, ricocheting off the overhang and humming near his head. He reloaded hastily, hearing MacSween pepper away with the short, flat report of his .32/20, and the dogs snarling and yapping, and the killers firing back ... and then the fire went out.

Kane estimated four of the six men were down.

But what of the two that were still alive?

He peered intensely downward, trying to spot them in the darkness, and saw spurts of rifle flame. The two were attacking MacSween! Kane levered a series of shots at the nearer of the two, and got in response a savage fire which showered the snow around him and threw clumps of ice up into his face. The man was a fine marksman! Kane sighted, and pulled the trigger on an empty gun.

Kane swore and whipped out his revolver. He supported his right hand with his left and shot. He shot again and again with almost a madness possessing him, and then an eerie silence fell over the battle scene, the only cry that of the dogs whining in the night. Kane listened, wondering why MacSween didn't shoot now. What was going on down there in the dimness ...?

'Skinny!' Kane shouted, loading his revolver quickly.

His call was lost in the snow and trees.

'Skinny!'

Now there were other sounds, new sounds, and the keening bark of dogs farther away. He emptied his revolver after the noises, knowing that the two survivors of the camp were escaping with their dogs.

'God damnit!' he yelled. "MacSween, answer me!'

There was no answer.

The thought that the old trapper was mortally injured or already dead down there was one he could not accept. Kane grasped the carbine and stuffed his revolver back inside the jacket, hastily put on the snowshoes, and stumbled and fell in his urgency to go below. He tore down a drift of loose, powdery snow, running breathlessly toward the dark, deserted camp site where only glowing coals of the fire provided a weak, almost useless illumination. He twisted around when he reached the valley, trying to orient himself to the scrub he'd seen from the overhang, the gloomy thicket where MacSween had been hiding.

'M-Morgan ...'

The gasping voice came from his left; Kane staggered for it, crashing into the woods. 'Skinny! Skinny, are you hurt?'

A vague, snow-covered shadow tried to get up, only to hunch over, moaning in obvious pain. 'Drag me ... in the snow, boy,' the weak, shaky voice requested. 'Drag me to the fire and stir it to burning. They ... they've gone now ...'

Kane drew his old trapper guide to the nearby sled, and then pushed the sled to the banked campfire. He rolled the dead killer who'd fallen in the embers off to one side, gagging slightly as he inadvertently saw the terribly burnt face and neck. He threw some branches on and stirred up the embers, and soon there was a roaring fire again. Then Kane went back to Skinny, who was lying on the sled, twisting slightly in his great pain.

'Where're you hit, Skinny?'

'In the thigh,' MacSween breathed. 'I ... I don't think anything's broken ... but try to stop the bleeding.'

Kane nodded, blanking from his mind the four corpses strewn about them. He took out his hunting knife and sliced MacSween's pants open along the right leg. A small, blue hole in the outside, upper leg was hardly bleeding at all, but the exit wound where the low-velocity slug had smashed through was larger and bleeding profusely. Still, there was no sign that a major artery or vein had been severed, for which Kane was extremely thankful.

'A clean one right through you,' Kane told MacSween with a forced smile as he cut a bandage from the pants. 'Hold the pad in place while I find something to bind it.'

He trussed the bandage to MacSween's leg with tourne-quet-tight strips of tarpaulin, and shortly afterward the bleeding stopped. Kane loosened the straps slightly to start circulation again, and then grinned down at his friend with a sigh of relief, noting the pale, dazed shock to MacSween's features but knowing the crisis was past. MacSween licked his blanched lips and tried to speak. 'Push me over between the fire and the overhang, boy, and stack the wood pile so I can reach it. Then you've got to——'

'Skinny,' Kane interrupted gently. 'You talk too much.'

'Damned if I don't, but if I'd been talking and lying low instead of getting up and seeing what I could do, I wouldn't have this hole through my leg now.' He chuckled dryly, some of the shock dissipating now in his rawhide-tough body, and he glanced around at the row of bodies. 'Find that devil Laverne, will you?'

Kane checked the dead marauders, and returned to MacSween shaking his head. "None of them are Laverne.'

'Yeah, yeah, so I see.' MacSween spat into the snow. 'The whites here are French-Canadians, those Quebec fellows I was telling you about. Half-blood bastards who deal with the Chippewas and always have the Mounties on their trail. What the hell are they doing this far south?'

Again Kane shook his head. 'They all look to be about thirty, and two of them look so much alike to've been twins.'

'They'd be the Farbe brothers,' MacSween grunted angrily. 'They got arrested ten years ago for selling whiskey to the Chippewas in Saskatchewan. Check their sleds, why don't you?'

Kane inspected the loads, finding the standard mountaineering supplies, rugs, a few skins, and eight metal cans holding about a gallon each. They sloshed when Kane shook them.

'Spirits?' MacSween asked.

'Might be.' Kane unscrewed the lid of one can and sniffed, his nose wrinkling from the pungent odor. 'Yep. And rawer than a new-born baby's bottom.'

'Haw!' MacSween said. 'Bring it here, boy. That's good against infection, y'know.'

'It's all of ten degrees out here, Skinny,' Kane argued. 'Whoever heard of infection in cold like this?'

'Now, you do not know what you are talking about!' MacSween rapped. 'Spirits are good for all sorts of ailments, including the cold! Give me that can, you whelp!'

Kane smirked and handed him the can. He watched the

old trapper take a healthy snort of the bad alcohol, then snap for air and blink the tears from his eyes. 'Whew!' MacSween coughed. 'It might not cure the bullet hole, boy, but it sure makes it a damn sight more tolerable to take!' He had another swallow, came up for air again, and went on: 'But look, you've got a passle of work to do. I'm going to need a lot of food and wood in easy reach, and you're going to have to put it there for me. Come tomorrow dawn, and you're going after them on your own. They can't travel far tonight; remember all they've taken along are the dogs and their weapons.

'Relax, Skinny,' Kane said. 'Get some sleep. I'm not about to leave you here by yourself.'

'The hell you're not!' MacSween retorted. 'You can't let them get away now! With wood, food, and this here medicine, I can hole up until spring, and damned if I haven't before! I've the Dakota record for it! Now, you do what I tell you—didn't your pappy ever teach you to respect your elders? Huh!'

Kane was startled by the old man's sudden ire, and was momentarily perplexed. He was worried about the wound and the chance of gangrene setting in, but on the other hand . . .

MacSween seemed to read Kane's mind, and the confusion that was in it. 'Don't be stupid, boy! I've had holes through me in the middle of winter before, and as long as bone and artery are intact, I'm in no danger. Don't worry—if I figured I needed help, I wouldn't be telling you to go. I ain't in any mood to commit suicide yet! But that's just the point, there isn't anything you can do for me here, not once you stack that wood and food nearby. Start, boy, *start*!'

Kane leaned over the old trapper, still feeling flustered and unsure. 'All right, Skinny. But let me tell you one thing. I don't want to go on without you, because I've met many fine men over the years, Skinny, but none of them are . . .'

He paused, the words choking up in his throat. He saw the blinking in MacSween's rheumy eyes, and turned away, unable to continue. Now there was more than simple pursuit which occupied Kane's thoughts, the fear rising in him that if he were killed, Skinny might become wolf-bait when the wood and food finally ran out. He silently vowed that he would return to this narrow, dark valley ... and that only his own death would stop him.

EIGHT

The dogs strained in their harness, their breaths gray crisp clouds after them, Kane trotting behind and calling encouragements to them. It was colder and windier this day, but the storm had cleared and the red burning sun colored the eastern ridges.

Behind lay the narrow valley where the fire burned high and bright for MacSween. Kane had left the old trapper wrapped inside several skins under the tarp; he'd left most of the equipment, taking along only an extra fur jacket, a pair of moccasins, food, some dry wood, a kitchen outfit, and two of the dead men's rifles—a short .44/40 carbine and a heavy buffalo rifle, calibre .50. They, along with his own Winchester and revolver gave him plenty of firepower.

The trail he followed was clearly outlined: tracks of *three* men (rather than only two as first supposed) and five or six dogs. The rest of the dogs were found in the woods, lashed to their harnesses. There wasn't enough food for all of them, and Kane was sadly forced to shoot them. Now, he allowed his own team to stretch out across the long, gently sloping grade, and the view he had was extensive all around him, as if he were on a prairie. In the distance were the wooded Black Hills and the six-thousand-foot ridge around Garrison Lake to the west, and Turtle Mountain was on his left now, indicating to him that he'd soon be over the border and into Canada.

Damn! He should have thought to've had Shane give him a letter of authority, at least a note of introduction! If the Redcoats or Mounties latched onto him and threw him in the can, he'd never be able to catch up to those thieving murderers! Well . . . he'd have to worry about that when it happened, he supposed, and pushed the worry from his mind for the moment.

The tracks headed straight north. MacSween had estimated he'd overtake the killers about mid-day, and now, with the sun high above the ridge in the east, Kane stared intently along the trail ahead. The reflection off the snow was ghastly, burning his eyes and making him remember the horrible times when sand had rubbed his lids raw during storms on the desert. Fearing snow-blindness, he pulled his cap down farther and made sure he closed his eyes at regular intervals to rest them.

Hours passed...

The sun was now in the west and throwing long shadows. Kane impatiently urged the team on, and then, abruptly, he spotted two dark points far ahead. The dogs! The men had made a special effort to bring some of their dogs along, for food and possibly defense as well. And now Kane recalled some other advice MacSween had given him that morning as he noticed the dark ridge rising up before him: try to reach the men before that ridge! Once there, they could hide in the terribly rugged growth and force Kane to leave his sled and chance a bullet in the back. 'Remember,' MacSween had instructed, 'that should they reach the ridge first, there is a wide, flat valley on the other side where the Pembina flows. And on the other side of that valley is the Canadian border fort, while toward the east is the trading post run by the bastards who sell spirits to the Chippewas.'

Kane, picturing this all in his mind, yelled to the dogs and urged them on faster. He could see two of the three men now, slaving away with three dogs apiece—were the dogs pulling them? He ranted and raved and swore at his team; he was getting closer to his hated enemies, but they were getting closer to the ridge. He pressed onward ... and then the men turned and stopped and pointed rifles at him. Short, smouldering shots cracked across the barren land.

'On!' he shouted, jerking from the sled the buffalo rifle. 'On, you dogs!'

Snow squirted beside and in front of him, and one bullet nearly lifted the cap off his head. He ignored the desperate fire, running forward and then suddenly falling flat in the snow on his stomach. He raised the mammoth gun and took aim. The recoil almost wrenched his shoulder off, but he grimly smiled as he watched one of the killers bloom a red flower in his chest and crash into the snow. The other man took one horrified look and ran for his life. Kane rammed a new lead ball in the gun, sighted down the long barrel, and pulled the trigger. The report was dry and hollow, and the second man stumbled and pitched forward, twitching, trying to creep toward the nearby ridge. Screams from him reached Kane as he rose up and began walking carefully to where the man was barely moving.

The first killer was lying on his back with sprawled legs and eyes stiffened with shock. Kane passed him, following a trail of blood now, and then he raised the rifle a third time, eyeing a thick neck twenty yards away. The man's coonskin cap flew off his head, which became no more but only a burst skull cracked like a nut hit by a sledgehammer.

Kane left both of them where they lay, returning to his dogs to quiet them. He fumbled around, rolling a bad cigarette, but the tobacco smoke felt warm and good in his lungs. His head felt abnormally hot; he took off his hat to allow the wind to cool it, then put it back on, his hands still quivering slightly. Two down, one to go—but it wasn't good enough.

Neither of the two had been the elusive Laverne.

The fact stuck in the Marshal's craw. MacSween had told him that morning: 'When you've gotten Laverne, take a good look around Pembina River. The Chippewas used to have their winter camps there, hunting otter, beaver, and moose. If you find empty camps, go to the Canadian fort and report, because it'll mean very bad trouble is going on. Whatever you do, don't start a one-man war up there ... and don't lose any sleep over me, I'll be growing fat and sassy down here ...'

So had said MacSween. But Kane had not gotten Laverne yet!

Kane tossed the butt of his cigarette into the snow, repacked the buffalo gun, and angrily got the dogs moving again. At least, there was still Laverne's track to follow ...

The sun was beginning its descent as Kane started his long climb up the ridge. He reached the crest and hiked along until he came to an open area where he could look down into the Pembina Valley. It stretched white and shiny in the late afternoon brilliance, a few blue shadows creeping up toward him in prophesy of the coming twilight. Thick growths of timber lined the river banks, and rising from them Kane could see squirrel-tails of smoke, about a mile of woods between each one. Kane remembered MacSween's words about the Chippewa camps ... and then came the recollection of how the smoke had risen from the massacred Crow camp! Was the same merciless slaughter repeating itself here?

And there, far to the north stretched a vast black smoke cloud heavy on the horizon. Dear God, was that the Canadian fort? But it *couldn't* be! It would mean these raiders must have a small army at their disposal!

But the smoke was there, and it was of the type generated by solid timber roasting slowly, the kind of timber from which a fort is built ... What in all hell was going on out here? Was there a civil war erupting in this outpost of civilization?

Kane's eyes stared eastward then, in the direction of the French-Canadian trading post. Would the answer be found there?

Kane sat down on the sled, dejected, and closed his eyes to contemplate what he should do. The shadows veiled the land and a pale moon rose in the sky, and after a long while, Kane stood up again and studied the terrain. He could dimly see a couple of naked hills across the mountain ridge, light blue beneath the stars and thin crescent of moon. His mind was made up now; he resolved to press on this very night, across the valley and in the direction of the trading post. He had no other choice.

With heavy heart, he rousted the dogs and started the long trek down into the slumbering Pembina Valley.

The hill was barren and oddly glistening in the moonlight, but Kane was hidden in the blanketing shadows at the edge of its woods. His Winchester was slung over his shoulder, and in his jacket were bullets to feed it, matches, and a bit of dried deer meat. Behind him was Turtle Mountain, its twelve thousand feet arching into the blue sky, the night stars forming over its conical summit like sparks flying from an active volcano.

The snow creaked beneath his snowshoes. The cold was like never-ending knives slicing through his flesh, the wind packing the new snow hard on top of the old. He could have traveled faster without his snowshoes, but MacSween had drummed a lesson of survival deeply into Kane's mind: never go without the shoes; you never can tell when the weather will change.

So Kane slogged along through the woods in his shoes, glimpsing occasionally the valley below, and a nearby staircase of ice where during the summer there'd be a flowing waterfall. On the other side of the frozen waterfall, he saw a series of dark huts, small fires flickering against the shadowed wood sides, and he heard muted voices of Indians, thick and eccentric as if very drunken.

Ah, a celebration! Kane grinned thinly and without humor; perhaps to celebrate their burning of the fort? And were those drums he heard as well, like faint heartbeats reaching up to him on the hill? Kane squatted for awhile, listening and staring at the fires and the vague outlines of the dark-skinned figures ... and then he began to slide forward carefully, slowly inching nearer the huts, the squeak of his snowshoes intolerably loud to his ears. He removed them, tied them together, and slung them over his shoulder after first sliding his carbine off and checking its action; he crept closer on soundless moccasins, rifle ready.

He dipped down in the hollow where the waterfall pooled; the sounds here were muted and fainter than before, but once up on the other side, they became stronger and distinct. The Chippewa's sharp barking war-chants sent icy shivers skating up his spine. He worked his way toward them like a cat, the ice in sharp relief from the moon and dancing fires, and finding a niche in the frozen water, he slipped into it to hide.

He was roughly fifty yards from the Chippewa huts now, and was able to count about thirty braves in buckskin coats and leggings staggering around the fires. The doors of the huts were wide open and more Indians came and went as if impervious to the freezing weather, and perhaps they were, for Kane caught the glimmer of metal cans in their hands—it was from here the spirits were coming!

Then, peering closely, Kane saw a sight which made his blood churn with heat. Across the main clearing there rose the crude timbers of a primitive gallows, four men dangling from rope-like straps. Their torsos were bare and covered with criss-crossed wounds, as if they'd been cruelly beaten and tortured before they were hung. Their pants were heavy cloth, brightly colored with stripes running down the outside seams—the trousers to uniforms, and Kane knew immediately that here were four Canadian soldiers, moaning and twisting, barely alive. The soldiers were strapped upside down, their heads dangling over a mighty bonfire crackling between the gallow posts.

Kane gritted his teeth together at the revolting scene before him. Were these the only survivors from Fort Pembina?

Then, as if in answer, two Indians came out of one of the huts, and others around them waved and shouted triumphantly. They started a chant which Kane could not translate, the two leaders pointing toward a small hillock just beyond the fiery glow and then running toward it, the rest of the braves at their heels, yelling louder than ever in their sing-song fashion. They stopped at the hillock, gathering around and then flinging back what looked to be a trapdoor to an earthen cellar.

Now something was being dragged from the cellar. No ... not something; *somebody*! A half-naked girl, blonde hair streaming around her shoulders, her clothing torn and hanging in long strips around her curvaceous body. The Indians forced her to stand between them, and the sight of the fire and their ear-trumpeting yells seemed to waken her from a drugged unconsciousness, for Kane saw her stiffen, lifting her head with stubborn pride and firm resolve. He watched, horrified, as she was hauled without mercy to the gallows, where she was unceremoniously hung in line with the soldiers, though left upright by her hands, rather than dangling by her legs. One of the Chippewas raised his hand, and a lean knife glittered wickedly in the dancing firelight.

The girl screamed, wrenching her bonds, but was forced to stand and view the Indian grasp one of the soldiers by his hair. Kane winced in helpless fury as he understood what was happening ... There was a roar of approval, and then the Indian raised a dripping scalp. The girl slumped forward, perhaps in a faint, but was slapped and again held upright.

Kane raised his rifle with shaking hands ... and then lowered it reluctantly. The few bullets he might be able to fire wouldn't have much effect one way or another—except to add another white man to those deadly gallows!

Another hoarse bellow, and another bloody scalp was raised in victory. Again the girl was forced to stand face to face with the grisly display. Kane thought that now the third soldier would be similarly butchered, but the Indians were more cruel with their torture, evidently deciding to let her meditate in terror and horror on what she'd seen and what would happen next. They untied her from the gallows, corded her hands behind her back, and led her to the cellar. She was thrown bodily back inside and the door slammed shut to the chorus of chanting laughter.

Kane hoped the two scalped soldiers were now dead and no longer in excruciating pain. They hung limply, blood streaming from their fleshless scalp and down into the fires directly below them. The Indians waved their scalps jeeringly into the faces of the remaining prisoners, and Kane felt admiration for the Canadian troopers' courage, for he was sure in their place, he'd be screaming his lungs out by now.

Nausea welled in his throat, and he had to swallow thickly to keep from becoming sick where he crouched. But another sight caught his attention, and his eyes narrowed with a cold, terrible hatred that turned his queasy stomach into a ball of ice. Out of the same hut from which the two Indians had come, now stepped an arrogant white man. Laverne!

The carbine shook in Kane's grip, his hate was so strong!

The Indians yelled and cheered their leader, dancing around him and lifting the scalps and knives they carried.

Kane shifted his eyes. He saw that the cellar where the girl was kept was momentarily unguarded, and unable to control his desire for action any longer, he began to creep forward again.

The soldiers at the gallows were screaming now, and the drums were beating louder and the Chippewa cries were stronger ... but Kane only heard this, for he was out of their sight as he edged his way around toward the far, dark side of the huts. Careful of each footfall, of each soundless step he made, the Marshal moved like a black spectre past the rear walls of the huts. Now he crouched as he went, not wanting to be spotlighted by the shafts of yellow illumination coming from the small back windows which was all the huts had. Slowly he worked down the scrub, keeping himself in the dark, still shadows.

A door slammed in one of the huts. Kane froze in his tracks, then wormed his way to the rear wall as he caught the all-too-familiar voice of his hated enemy, Laverne. He pressed his ear to the cold wood, listening intently.

'...Could be an advantage,' another man was saying now in a nasal, sing-song voice. 'The redskins get all the blame and the Mounties will fight them, not us. They'll never suspect us at all! That is, unless they somehow learn we're behind it.'

And now Laverne spoke, hard and sharp. 'Pshaw! Who's going to tell them? Half an hour from now and the last soldiers will be dead, and in less than a month the ice will be breaking up. When we move on then, there'll be nobody in all of Beaver Creek or Beaver Valley to stop us!'

Beaver Creek! Kane thought of the ruins of Three Crow's spartan cabin ... and then of Beaver Creek with its Crow camp. What was it these murderers were after? And why must it start after the ice began to loosen? Kane strained to catch their words ... but the hut wall was thick, and he could only pick up snatches of the conversation over the noise of the drunken Chippewas ...

'...no mistake,' he heard a third man say. 'The tests ...'

'...control? Do they get more spirits now ... us too ...'

Laverne's voice rumbled through to Kane: 'In a couple

of hours they'll all be asleep. Then we can get the hell out of here without being noticed . . .'

Kane shook his head, frustrated and bitterly cold from staying in this one position too long. And there was the girl to consider . . . He crawled from the wall and back into the scrub, angling around toward the sunken cellar. Close by, Indians were lurching unsteadily, their speech garbled with liquor, and others were already passed out and snoring on the frozen ground. The air was fetid with the stench of smoke, blood, and the bad alcohol.

He reached a dimly lit spot where he could see the corner of the hillock where the trapdoor lay. He removed his snowshoes, and then figuring that his clothes were similar enough to the skins the Indians were wearing, he took off his cap and let his long, sweaty hair hang down. He slipped the cap in his jacket and crept closer to the cellar on his stomach, the snowshoes underneath him.

Reaching the cellar door, he could see the entire camp in full detail. The Chippewas had momentarily forgotten the men dangling from the gallows, and were dancing and drinking around the fires, shouting, chanting, and thumping their drums. A hut door opened and Laverne stepped out . . . Kane pressed himself to the earth, fingering his carbine. If he were caught, Laverne would die with him!

But Laverne disappeared again inside the hut, and Kane breathed a sigh of relief. He wriggled the trapdoor up a bit, then gently eased it back so it wouldn't squeak. He prayed the girl wouldn't suddenly scream as the light streamed in, but would remain stoically brave as she'd been before . . . The thought of those gallows and the slicing knives worried him greatly, and it took a moment for him to stop the inadvertent shivering that rippled through his flesh.

Then, stretching his arm down inside the cellar for support, he twisted himself over the lip of the sill and slid eel-like down inside. The trapdoor rested heavily on his back, pressing down and making him kick his feet. Then he was all the way in, turning around so he could gradually ease the door back into its closed position. The light was suddenly gone, and it was totally black.

'Oh! Oh!' he heard a hysterical voice whimper, and

almost frantically he called back: 'For God's sake, don't scream!'

There was immediate silence. Had she fainted? Then:

'Who ... who's there?'

The cellar was small, dank, and the girl was close by him. He turned toward the halting voice, whispering: 'A friend. Do exactly what I tell you, and we might get out of here alive.'

'Oh God,' she moaned, 'if only ... But, but *who* are you? You don't sound like a Canadian.'

'U.S. Marshal Kane, Ma'am. You might say I'm a little bit farther north than usual. Now look, I'll go first, and when I'm out of the cellar, you stick out your hands and I'll pull you free. Let the door slide along your body, but don't let it fall whatever you do! Is that clear?'

'Y-Yes. But I'm tied up.'

Kane groped in the darkness until he found her, and then cut the thongs which bound her wrists. Then he located the trapdoor again and raised it gently, inch by inch. The dancing was even more abandoned now, and none of the Indians looked as if they were in any condition to see what he was doing, even if they'd been interested. He slipped through, rolled over, and caught the slender white arms which were already showing. He pulled the girl up out of the cellar in one long gliding tug, knowing his quickness was hard on her, but realizing there was no alternative. She caught the door agilely with her heels, allowing it to settle back in place without a murmur ... and then they were in the scrub, hunching down in the shadows behind the huts.

The girl was close to collapse. He stripped off his jacket and placed it around her bare shoulders as she slipped her arms through the oversized sleeves. She sagged against him then with a muffled sob, and he held her closely, comfortingly, not minding the cold which sliced through his woolen shirt. After a few moments of rest, he emptied the pockets of his jacket and filled his shirt with the extra ammunition, then said to her:

'You know where the waterfall is?'

Before she could answer, there came a sudden noise of

approaching footsteps. He forced her down beside the wall, and unsheathing his long hunting knife, he stealthily approached the corner of the hut.

A Chippewa was staggering with one of the cans in his hand. His head was rolling foolishly on his dirty neck as he wobbled toward Kane. Kane hissed, attracting the Indian's drunken attention; the brave murmured something slovenly, taking another long swallow from the can, and then staggering for the deep pocket of shadows in which Kane hid. When he was close enough, Kane reared up in front of his startled eyes and drove the knife to its hilt into his chest. The Indian died without a sound. Kane grasped the folding body and eased it down, then rolled it over on its stomach to make it appear as if it was a simple case of a drunk passing out ... and then Kane returned to the girl, feeling no remorse in his heart for the death.

The girl was shivering, her head buried in her hands. Kane whispered to her low and intense: 'Hear me! You must go up the slope behind here and to the waterfall. Once there, cross the falls and go up the valley to the edge of the woods there. I have a sled parked next to three huge oaks—they stand out like signs, and you won't be able to miss them. You'll find clothes there. Drive the sled farther up into the woods to where there's an overhang that doesn't have any trees growing on it. Now, you've got that? You want me to repeat the instructions?'

'N-No ...'

'Can you handle a dog team?'

'A ... little bit ...'

'Well, do your best. I'll follow your tracks and come after you. Remember: past the waterfall, the trees, and the overhang. Now, get going!'

He heard a slight whimper and a moan, and then she was scurrying through the scrub in the direction he'd indicated. Kane nodded and sighed, then worked back to the corner where his carbine was propped against the wall. The smell of the dead Indian was strong and bitter in his nostrils. He noticed the can which the brave had dropped, and picking it up, he found it was still about three-quarters full of the obnoxious alcohol. He began splashing the liquid on the hut, especially up around the roof, and then moved to the other ones. With the remaining liquor, he doused the cellar's trapdoor and gallow's frame, and now the cold had eaten through his shirt, paralyzing his arm. He drank the last half-inch in the can, and the alcohol warmed his insides as if he'd been walloped with a mallet. MacSween was right! The stuff did cure the cold for awhile!

Kane hunkered down behind the huts again, wishing he had another can to squirt around the dwellings. Half the Indians were passed out on the snow, and he swore that he'd have poured the can on them as well! He waited a little longer until he'd estimated the girl had gotten a half-hour's head start, and then he fumbled in his pockets for some matches.

His fingers could hardly move any more, and his teeth were chattering like castanets. But he managed to light one, and sheltering it with the palm of one hand, he placed it to the bark of the nearest roof, sodden now with the alcohol.

The flame caught with a greedy snap, and in a few seconds the entire wall was crackling in flames. Kane clutched his rifle and ran up the steep slope after the girl as fast as he could, hearing behind him the complete village blossoming into fire. He also heard screams of terror and yells of outrage, and now shots were being fired in all directions. He topped the rise and glanced back: the huts were infernoes, and the flames had spread to the gallows and cellar. He emptied his carbine into the hysterically milling crowd of Indians, and was pleased to see three more of the heartless killers stagger and drop.

Out of one burning cottage spilled the three white men he'd overheard. One pointed up the slope, and they all turned to stare his way; Kane reloaded, sighted, and dropped the one who was pointing, and the other two dived for cover. One of the two was Laverne, and Kane chased the man with bullet after bullet, cursing himself when Laverne dropped from sight, still unharmed. The devil must have charmed that bastard's life!

But there was bitter consolation in the sight of the three sleds burning brightly, as the hut they were parked next to fell in ruins over them. It was some small payment for what had happened at Beaver Creek and Cheyenne River, though not nearly enough. He hoped he'd have another chance to even the debt, and turning his back on the camp, Kane began the long journey to his sled and the girl he'd rescued.

NINE

Kane was bone-stiff with cold by the time he reached the treeless overhang. He glanced over his shoulder at the valley, smiling grimly as he saw much of it illuminated from the savage flames of the dying camp. He could spot small figures running around in confusion and terror, drunk cries drifting up faintly, along with the bark of rifles.

He turned away and began running along the overhang, wondering where the girl was. He'd been following her tracks up to the large oaks, and from there, the trail of the sled and dogs ... She should be right around here, waiting for him, but there was no sign of her or his sled, only the never-ending tracks. And now, under the overhang where the snow was not crusted and packed by the freezing wind, Kane noticed for the first time that he was without his snowshoes! Damnation! In his haste and concentration, he'd forgotten them back at the Chippewa camp!

He had barely enough breath left to swear, but swear he did, low and profanely. He shuffled on through the powdery drifts, the trail easy to follow in the moonlight and reflected fire. Then, glancing higher, he saw the girl awkwardly driving the sled toward the mountain ridge, and soon he could hear the dogs and her high-pitched voice urging them faster. Then they all seemed to waver and stumble, coming to a grinding halt, and Kane was able to catch up after about ten minutes of heavy trotting.

The dogs were tangled in a spruce thicket, and the girl was moaning, on the verge of tears. He loosened the dogs first, unable to speak because his wind was gone, and when they were once again straightened out, he turned to her in exasperation. She was dressed as he'd last seen her, wearing hardly anything except his great fur jacket.

'You little fool!' he snapped. 'I told you to get some clothes out of the sled and dress yourself warmly.

She stared up at him, misery watering her eyes. 'I ... I only wanted to get away. I d-didn't want to stop, not for anything. I ... I'm so afraid!'

'Huh!' he snorted, and began digging through the supplies on the sled. He found another jacket and a set of extra pants and thrust them at her. 'Put them on and be quick about it,' he ordered with more sharpness than he actually felt toward her.

She nodded, handing back his own jacket, which was delightfully warm from her body and made him sigh with contentment when he slipped it back on. He helped her dress, rolling up the oversized pants and clinching the thick belt extra tight around her slender waist. The excitement of the fire was still beating heavily in his heart, the blood pounding in his head after the long, gruelling run to here; his hands quivered with eagerness, but she didn't say anything, didn't ask anything.

'Ready?' Kane asked. 'Okay. You hold onto the bars behind the sled and call out if you start getting too tired.' He roared at the dogs, and the dogs heeded his urgent command, throwing themselves in the harness.

Kane trotted alongside, silently trying to anticipate what Laverne would do now. The Indians had been soddenly drunk, and were probably in no condition to hunt them till morning—if then! There'd been three whites, one of them down and possibly dead, and their sleds were badly damaged. Would Laverne and the other man try to track them down on foot? Or was there a reserve sled and supplies Kane was not aware of?

Laverne would be after them, there was no question in Kane's mind about that. It was simply a matter of how soon. Time was of the essence, and he had to exploit every minute given them ... but how long could the girl last? Her rescue had probably given her a boost of hope and courage, but it would soon dissipate and she'd collapse in fatigue and shock. And then ...?

They crossed the Pembina Valley in the moonlight, Kane frequently looking back for any sign of pursuers. The sky behind them had a pink tinge to it, indicating the fire he'd set was still raging uncontrolled.

'On!' he shouted at his team. 'On, on!'

But they slowed while the valley ended and sloped up into a slanting ridge. Kane had to untangle the harness time and again, and he could see the girl sagging in the bows, her legs buckling beneath her from weariness.

'Can you hold out a little longer?' he panted, and she nodded heavily. Once more he set the dogs to running, hoping they could cross the ridge and move down the other side to the flat, prairie-like level. Then she could sit on the sled and rest. 'On, you damned dogs! On . . .!'

The snow proved treacherous to his plans. There was a hidden crevice, concealed by the shadows, and before any warning could be had, the sled nosed into the hole and tipped over. The girl was sent sprawling in the snow, and two of the dogs were pinned beneath the sled before Kane could get to it. The dogs whined miserably when he released them, and tried to crawl away, their hind legs and perhaps their backs broken and shattered. Kane cut them free of the pack and reached for his revolver. Then he thought about the sound of a shot . . . and took out his knife instead.

The girl was sitting up, not making a sound as he killed the two dogs. He went to her, and his voice was blurred and congealed in his throat. 'Come on,' he said. 'Onto the sled.'

'I . . . can't.'

'You *have* to, damnit!' Kane helped her to her feet and started her toward the sled. 'We can't stay here.'

Her legs crumpled as if made of paper. 'I am . . . I am so cold!'

Kane stared down at her, and then out over the level and the oval of black forest far beyond. They'd never reach it . . . but they had to or die! 'Look, there's only four or five miles left to go. Try . . . Try, and you'll make it.'

'No, I can't.' Her eyes closed and she began to mewl.

Kane slapped her cheeks with his mittened hand, then shook her shoulders roughly. 'You weak-kneed woman! Give up like this! Ain't worth the bother of saving!'

His feigned contempt worked. Suddenly flushed and

shamed, she bristled, her eyes flashing angrily. 'How *dare* you...!'

'I calls them as I sees them, Ma'am,' Kane said with the same harshness. 'Prove me wrong. Or do I kick you all the way?'

Furious now, she staggered upright and to the sled, grasping the frame while Kane got the remaining dogs to their feet. There were only four now and they looked very, very tired and bedraggled.

'On!' he shouted at them, and the girl was almost swept off her feet as the sled jerked on its way again. They went down the slope at a furious clip, and then the sled got stuck again and the dogs went end over end in their lines. Kane warmed the air with his oaths while he unscrambled the dogs and righted the sled, uncaring if he were blistering a lady's ears. They floated on over the powdered drifts once again, and the woods opened out into the barren level.

'Soon there!' he called out encouragingly, staring across the moon-sparkling waste. 'Hang on—for King and country!'

The girl stumbled to keep up with the flying sled, Kane beside it and pushing it along to help the dogs a little. And when the dogs faltered in their weariness, he would curse them brutally and kick them to move again, showing no mercy. Twice he had to pause to pick the girl up, and the last half-mile she lay draped over the tarpaulin, flopping with exhaustion. But he never stopped once, not even to rest his own flagging body, not until he'd reached the safety of the deep, overgrown forest.

There in its protection he called a halt, and the dogs sunk down as if they'd been shot. Behind him the long valley was crystal and magic in the moonlight, the ridge from whence they'd come a black, massive wall in the distance. It was here they'd have to camp, for better or worse, and mind made up he urgently set to work. He hauled the panting dogs over to a thicket of spruce and kicked up the crust so they could burrow beneath the snow.

He returned to the sled and found the girl with her head down on the tarp, and for a moment he wished he could follow her example. It was well below zero, perhaps by as much as thirty degrees, and the cold ate through him, sapping his energy. Even standing upright, he felt a sleepiness crawling up him, the aching desire to rest in this numbing cold, just for a little while ...

He jerked himself awake and reached for her.

'Don't fall asleep now!' he yelled in her ear. 'You'll die if you do! Are you listening to me? Are you listening?' He shook her until her head rattled. 'Keep awake! Keep awake!'

And when her eyes were half open again and she was sitting up, he began to make camp for them. He trampled flat a small circle and dug the loose snow out with his hands. His back ached, but he steeled himself to the task, not stopping until the moss and grass showed. He shook the girl some more and took the axe from the sled, cutting limbs of spruce from which to form a bed on the bare ground. Then he cut blocks of snow rigid enough to be called ice, stacking them around the bed to form a low wall. He felled the spruce trees from which he'd taken the limbs and roofed over the bed with them, some more branches, and then a layer of loose snow. When he was finished, he dug out a small opening and then returned to the sled to fetch the girl, some dry wood, and the bundle of supplies.

He all but had to drag the girl to the enclosure. After she'd crawled inside, he made a few more trips to the sled, threw the dogs some scraps of meat, and took blankets and the tarp inside his little ice house with him.

He pawed a hole in the floor and built a small wood-chip fire by the entrance. More wood was carefully added until he had a pleasant blaze going, and then he quickly unrolled the bundle of supplies for the rock-hard meat and some cans of beans. He warmed the meager food, pleased as the temperature slowly rose in his hollow, and when the food was ready, he thrust the skillet toward the girl and handed her a spoon.

'Eat!' he commanded.

A heavy eyelid fluttered. She stared dreamily at the beans and cube of meat, taking the spoon as if she didn't know what to do with it. Slowly she began to eat, and while she was, Kane went back outside to look around. No light showed through the snow and spruce. He chopped down a tall, dry spruce and broke it up into smaller pieces, carrying the logs back inside. Then he cut another block of ice and wedged it in the opening after him. They were both sealed in now.

It was actually cosy inside, he thought, the firelight shimmering off the block walls and the odor of fresh spruce sharp and spicy, fragrant with the mixture of smoke, beans, and the meat. Smiling, he turned back to the girl and was happy to see she'd licked the skillet clean.

'Good girl!' he told her, and put the rest of the food in the pan to cook. He hummed quietly to himself, watching her crawling under the blankets, and she looked back at him, eyelids drooping but with a curious wakefulness to her eyes.

Kane ate his dinner, not caring if it burned his tongue. His body had an insatiable need for warmth and nourishment, and it had been too long a time since he'd had either. He cleaned the skillet and packed it away, then unsheathed his hunting knife. The girl whitened, pulling herself backward against the wall.

Kane ignored her frightened actions, boring a hole in the northern wall large enough to slip his arm through. He could see the entire plateau they'd crossed, all the way to the black ridge. The plateau itself was brilliantly pale under the moon and stars, but it was a diamond-blue, cold light which made distances and figures tricky to judge. Kane took one more scan of the region, then closed the hole with a ball of snow.

He turned to the girl then and said, 'Are you very cold?'

'No. But I feel sort of funny. My feet . . .'

Kane crossed to her and removed her shoes. She tried to protest but he hushed her with one solid glare, and then he studied her feet, finding them like waxed ivory. He pinched their toes. 'Feel anything?'

'No . . .'

'They're frostbitten,' he told her and began to rub them, twisting and slapping them so hard that she had to grit her teeth and lean back on both hands. Kane got warm from the exertion and took off his cap, his shaggy black hair falling down in his eyes. He worked at her feet until the skin turned a light pink and she was making little squeaking noises to show she was feeling pain. 'Oh! Oh, that hurts!' she yelped, the circulation returning and her nerves reviving. 'Oh! Oh, ouch!'

'You sound like one of the dogs,' Kane said with a laugh. 'Tell me, can you——'

'Oh! Oh yes, very well now, thank you!'

He stopped then with a nod, and there followed a short, uncomfortable moment of silence. It made him feel uneasy the way she stared at him, at his untidy black hair as if he were another form of savage. At last, her eyes casting downwards, the girl began to speak in a low, faltering tone.

'I . . . I guess I should thank you, Marshal. You saved my life. I . . . I'm Valerie Fremont, *Mrs* Fremont. My husband John is—was—next-in-command at Fort Pembina.' Her voice dragged and was monotonous, as if she was forcing herself to recited a hated school lesson. 'There was some trouble, Indian trouble, and the commandant rode away with most of the garrison. My husband was left in charge of a fifteen-man detachment. Then *they* came . . .'

'Who're *they*, Mrs Fremont?'

'The Indians, the Chippewas. The trouble had all been a lure, a trick to weaken the fort. They came in the night, shooting and firing flaming arrows, and yelling, always yelling, yelling . . .'

'Stop it!' Kane snapped, shaking her severely.

Valerie shuddered and then straightened, her eyes clearing. 'They shot John in the doorway of our house, Marshal. I . . . can see him now, falling inside the hall, and those awful beasts jumping over him, trampling over his body and dragging me out in the snow. Most everybody was dead. There were so few of us left.'

She lapsed into a painful silence, and after a moment, Kane asked her: 'Were these the Chippewas who camp along the Pembina?'

'Oh no! They're peaceful,' she answered, shaking her head. 'These were strangers, I think from around Winnipeg or Saskatchewan. They burned their own people's camps, the ones along the river, and I heard how the innocent children and women screamed.'

'And Laverne?' Kane pressed, putting on her wet moccasins. 'Do you know of this man?'

'Very well,' she said acidly. 'He's a trader from the south, never up to any good, and John tried for a long time to have him barred from the Territory. John suspected him of selling whiskey and spirits to the Chippewas, but the commandant, Captain Faucher, would never believe it.'

'Why not?'

Valerie's head was beginning to nod again, her eyes glazed and oddly filmed. 'Faucher is French-Canadian ... never could believe wrong of his heritage ... never could, and now ... now ...'

Her head fell forward. Kane grasped her by her fine blonde hair and forced her to look at him.

'When are the soldiers returning, Mrs Fremont? Valerie? When is Captain Faucher returning to the fort?'

'About ... a few days ... I don't know ...'

Kane let go of her and put more wood on the fire. He noticed that his arms moved as if encased in mud, and his own eyes refused to stay open. 'Valerie,' he said in a thick, sleepy voice. 'Valerie, listen to me ...'

'Mmmmm?'

'The fire will die out while we're asleep. I've only one bag; we'll have to share it or we'll freeze to death tonight. Do you hear me?'

'Yes ... Yes, I'm listening ...'

Kane rolled out the sleeping bag on the tarpaulin and unbuttoned it. He placed more logs on the fire and then rolled the young widow onto the bag, and after one more quick inspection through the hole in the wall, crawled in beside her and fastened the bag closed.

They lay face to face. She was shivering, the fire and food unable to warm her entirely. Kane hesitated ... then opened her jacket and his own, wrapping them around them on the outside for additional warmth. The few clothes she had on were tattered rags, no more than wispy decoration for her vibrant body naked underneath. Her round, high breasts were hard like frozen apples, and pressed deeply against his chest as she snuggled closer in automatic reflex. Their thighs touched, moved together. But Kane was too exhausted to take notice, not even as her breasts warmed and became pliant with promise. He yawned, holding her close to him as she breathed deeply and rhythmically . . . and then he drifted into an unconsciousness, a sleep untroubled by dreams, worries, or desires . . .

TEN

Valerie Fremont awoke slowly, unsurely, her mind not focusing at once as to where she was. Her first sensation was that of warmth, and it seemed to her the most pleasant warmth she'd ever experienced. Her eyes opened then, and she couldn't see anything except a mass of dark hair lying across a strange man's face. She heard the man's regular, deep breathing and felt it against her cheeks—and suddenly the recollections of all that had happened returned with crystal clarity.

She turned her head away, sucking in her breath. Now, staring above her, she saw light filtering through the frigid walls, and the ice on the spruce roof where their breaths had condensed and caked. More consciousness returned, and now the young widow realized how she was lying in the sleeping bag, stretched out against the man and almost naked. Had she...? No, *he* must have undressed her, and after an initial moment of fear, her heart calmed and she realized why he had done so. She looked at him again, this American, this Marshal Kane who had rescued her from torture and death ... and it seemed to her that asleep, he appeared much younger and somehow tender.

How old was he? Probably in his late thirties. She studied Kane's relaxed features, noticing his black, bushy eyebrows and once-broken nose and the scars that indicated the battles he'd fought—and won. The hard, taut manner to him was softened in sleep, the lines of his peaceful face attractive and having character, even though his beard was scraggy and his hair was matted and wet. She thought fleetingly that in his own territory, around his own home, he probably didn't have a beard and his hair would be properly combed...

What thoughts! She stiffened, abruptly wishing not to be so close to Kane, and she twisted in the bag to get away.

His eyes opened, all at once and with sharp intensity.

She heard herself say: 'How did you *dare* to ...!' And then she stopped, knowing the foolishness of her own words.

He didn't reply, turning instead to the snow wall and the feeble light which percolated through the blocks. The fire was burnt down, almost out, and their breaths were frosty before them. Finally he asked: 'Did you sleep well? Are you still very cold?'

She struggled again, and nodding as if he understood, he undid the row of buttons along the side of the bag. She got up, wrapping the coat around her lightly clad body, and the words of prim respectability and reprimand jumped to her tongue again. She swallowed them, knowing modesty was a luxury in a situation like this ... a liability, in fact, which could kill her as sure as the Indians. Ashamed at her prissy reactions, she smiled faintly down at Kane and said:

'Yes. I ... slept just fine, and was very warm, thanks to you.'

Kane smiled back. 'Good. Can you get the fire burning again while I look around outside? We're going to need food and warmth before we can continue.'

The thought of endless stretches of bitter cold depressed her, but Valerie immediately went to the embers, setting to work to rebuild the blaze. She watched Kane remove the block at the entrance hole ... and then he was crawling out and was gone.

The cold hit Kane like a massive iron fist. The dawn was blue and frozen, as if too weak to become the day. The spruces around him stood tall and motionless in the stationary air, the only sound the crunch of the snow-crust beneath his moccasins. Kane went to the sled and stared northward, toward the ridge.

The plateau spread white and virginal, nothing moving across its frozen expanse, and the ridge seemed quiet and deserted, not even showing signs of smoke. Kane returned and saw that Valerie had gotten a fine fire burning, and he started to make coffee from the melting icicles dripping from the roof. They shared the same mug, and over its rim, Kane could see that the night's rest had done her well, her eyes no longer red and swollen and her cheeks showing color. She was beautiful, he thought; beautiful and brave and hardy ...

He said: 'We should eat something before we go.'

'I'm really not hungry, Marshal Kane.'

He couldn't help grinning at her. 'That's awfully formal, Valerie, and I'm not marshal of anything up here in Canada. Call me Morgan.'

'Morgan? That's a nice name.' She repeated it slowly: 'Morgan...' And then she blushed, remembering the night's intimate position, and hurriedly started preparing food.

Shortly afterward they were breaking camp and packing the sled. The dogs came out, shaking themselves free of the snow and snarling around as they usually did, and Kane harnessed them to the sled and pulled it from the spruce scrub. The going was slow at first, and Kane had to help push across the sticky snow until he was gnashing his teeth with frustration.

But by the time the sun's red eye was up over the ridge, they were through the worst of the forest and making better time. Valerie trotted beside the sled while Kane pushed and called to the team: 'On! On, you mangy devils!'

The thought of Laverne behind him and MacSween waiting ahead seemed to pull Kane forward with urgency. 'On! On!'

They passed the chewed corpses of the two men Kane had shot with the buffalo rifle, lots of fox and wolf tracks all around their remains. Kane steered well around them, but Valerie glanced back with agitated curiosity.

'What was that?' she asked hesitantly.

'Wolves,' he answered, and that was all.

The treetops raised across the plateau, and Kane pulled up to grin at Valerie, saying with a sigh: 'We'll soon be there!'

But behind them, on the other side of the forest where their little ice-block hut still stood, one, two ... no *three* men with dog-team and sled were crossing the plateau after them, closing in with astonishing speed.

Kane drove the sled through the narrow valley gorge at breakneck haste, afraid ... afraid he would not be in time. He was sure of it, positive he was too late as he spied the now familiar mountain wall ... but then he caught the faint, lazy trail of blue-gray smoke, and he breathed with relief. Skinny was alive!

MacSween was very much alive.

'By all that's holy!' he yapped when the dogs came charging back into his camp. He stared wondrously at the girl beside Kane, blinking at her blonde-haired beauty clothed in shapeless skins.

'Skinny!' Kane called to him. 'Skinny, how are you?'

'Fine,' the old trapper replied, 'but damned good you came when you did.'

Kane looked at MacSween, seeing how the old man was sitting up with his Winchester across his knees. 'What's the matter?'

'All that shooting must've disturbed a hibernating grizzly,' MacSween explained. 'Ol' bruin came down here preparing to have me as his meal, and I throwed a shot and half the fire at him before he routed. I think he's winged—but I *know* he's out there, hungrier than a ... well, a bear, damnit, and I haven't been able to sleep a wink. But where the tunket did you meet up with this here squaw, Morgan?'

Kane related what had happened in terse, abbreviated sentences while he inspected MacSween's wound. The bullet holes had closed and were knitting nicely, no sign of infection or gangrene.

'I told you so,' MacSween said, and then snapped waspishly: 'If you're finished showing my nekkid body in front of this young lady, we best be off for Dawson's. We've got to warn him and the sheriff at Jamestown!'

They loaded the sled with the rest of the supplies, adding tinned food, dried meat, and fish for the dogs, some extra harness, sleeping bags, and extra clothing. Kane placed MacSween on the sled, packed in skins and the tarpaulin, and placed the Winchester in the old trapper's firm grip. Valerie

Fremont followed Kane's feverish preparations with quiet eyes. She had seen the four dead bodies in the snow here, and remembered the two back along the valley, and thought over Kane's short explanation of his actions. Suddenly she knew the kind of man he was—and where she'd heard of him before!

It had been in the Winnipeg *Globe*. The newspaper had reported a fight—no, a war in a small Arizona town called Tombstone. Marshal Kane had been in the thick of it, accounting for himself with honor and courage...

'Mrs Fremont, Ma'am,' Skinny said to her when everything was ready. 'One question before we leave—what kind of people lived around your husband's fort?'

'Farmers, mostly. They've gone now, I'm sure of it.'

'Well, we'll raise a stink when we get to Dawson's,' promised MacSween, 'that'll pay back in token the massacre of the fort. Beggin' your pardon, Mrs ... I mean, with your husband, I mean...'

'I understand,' she said softly. 'Thanks.'

It was still hard for her to believe what had happened to her, the tragic events like some kind of foggy dream. The burning and looting and killing ... the yelling Indians ... and scalps brandished in front of her ... the whole affair was so completely insane! So totally unexpected after the boring routine of the border fort! She really hadn't accepted yet the fact that she was a widow and the life she'd known gone forever, replaced by wild flights through frozen tundra, snarling dogs, and two bearded men in furs. Especially the one man, Marshal Kane—Morgan—who'd appeared out of nowhere when she was sure she was to be raped and scalped, and who was bringing her out of the nightmare and into clothes, warmth, and food ... Yes, and into a new place, a new life—and scared loneliness.

But Valerie was not a stranger to the Northwestern wilderness. Her father had been a colonel in Quebec's main infantry division, so the frozen valleys and windswept peaks were in her blood. This was the first time she'd met the land as an enemy, though, and where she'd gotten the strength to resist and fight it was beyond her to know. But she had, and she was resolved not to falter now. The world of husband John, the other officers' wives, and the social life at the fort were rapidly disappearing in the face of the obstacles ahead. Now her world consisted of icy mountains and an injured old trapper, and Marshal Morgan Kane . . .

'Head through the valley, boy,' MacSween ordered as they set off at a quick trot. 'I'm hoping the grizzly is farther up in the hills, nursing his wounds.'

'All right.' Morgan couldn't have cared less about a starving grizzly bear accidentally rooted from its hibernation. He was totally concerned about the deadly race ahead of them. Thank God Skinny was alive! Now he could concentrate solely on the long trek itself and leave the navigation to his friend. Ah . . . but there was the additional worry he had about Valerie, for how long could the young woman last out here? And the depleted team could never manage two on the sled; the dogs were having a hard enough pull as it was with just MacSween loading them down!

Kane steered the sled through the dark valley as MacSween directed. Each swerve of the sled made the wounded trapper grit his teeth together in wincing pain, and Kane knew MacSween's thigh was still far from healed. But there was never the slightest complaint from MacSween, only the urging to go on faster, faster . . .

Unknown to them, however, the enraged grizzly bear was not high in the hills, but less than half a mile away from them. It was seven and a half feet high and its three hundred and fifty pound body was lean and sinewy from lack of food. And in search of food, its red, drooling jaws snapped and growled, and its beady eyes were yellow with fury. The scent of the hated human was thick in his nostrils, and now there were other scents, of two more. Lurching on great-clawed feet, he bounded toward them . . .

Kane heard the howls and automatically reached for his Winchester packed on the sled. The dogs were wild with fright, untamed, and throwing the sled into confusion. He tried to control its skidding direction, but then the sled went over on its side sending MacSween toppling into the snow and Valerie screaming. Kane turned in the direction of the hellish growls, levering the rifle.

And the lever stuck half-way!

The cold had jammed the mechanism! And now the bear was on them, and because Kane was the closest—and because Kane was the one who moved—it attacked the Marshal. It came tearing at him, huge hairy arms extended and massive fangs dripping with blood-lust, and Kane stumbled backward, trying desperately to unfreeze the lever. He moved away from the sled, away from Skinny and Valerie Fremont, seeing the beast's thick belly and the swiping paws closing in.

Kane danced out of the way once, twice ... and then he was in a patch of clear, powdery snow, dropping down in it up to his hips. The bear actually leaped at Kane, and Kane thrust himself sideways, driving the carbine up against the wide-mouthed jaws. The teeth closed—and suddenly there was no more stock to the Winchester! Again the bear tried to tackle him in the snow, and again Kane miraculously swerved aside, crawling with everything he had through the drift. The bear pursued him relentlessly, and his heavy, furry pads were better suited for the snow than Kane's slim moccasins.

What was it that Skinny was yelling?

A claw swiped his jacket, tearing a long rent in the fur, and then Kane made sense of what his old trapper friend was frantically telling him. He reached for his revolver, the pea-shooter MacSween had disdained. A Colt against a grizzly? Madness! Kane aimed quickly at the red jaws as the bear attacked again. The shot snapped, and a spurt of blood gushed from the monstrous face. The bear bellowed in rage and pain and clawed at the jutting spruce stump that was on his right. A strip of flesh had been torn free where the bullet had ejected; the flap hung down in the animal's way, and he snatched at it as if it were a strange little creature antagonizing it, steps stumbling and crashing through the snow crust.

Kane twisted his leg on some hardy scrub and fell backward in the drifts. The bear lumbered toward him, still pawing at his flap of skin but more intent on eating this human than ever before. Kane knew he couldn't escape the beast this time, and in desperation, straightened his right arm and emptied the revolver directly into the bear's leering face and chest.

One—two—three—four—and the bear jerked with each impact and blood poured from gaping holes like crimson fountains. Kane lay beneath the huge shadow of the tremendous beast, seeing it quiver as if with fever, the yellow eyes dimming. Then Skinny's Winchester barked, and the bear shuddered as the bullet smashed into its thick skull behind its left ear. The grizzly swayed . . . and then keeled over like a fallen tree, quaking the earth where it fell and totally mashing a spruce scrub beneath it.

Kane lay where he was for a moment, the shock still too great in him to allow his muscles to operate. Then gradually he got up, afraid he would fall back down, and stumbled almost drunkenly toward the sled.

'I'll never say a thing about that pop-gun again,' Skinny swore, and his lined face was gray with anxiety beneath his beard. Tears were running down Valerie Fremont's cheeks, and she began crying openly now that the actual danger was over, frozen panic melting into weeping relief. Kane looked from one to the other, and then managing a feeble grin, began to reload his pistol.

'I think I'll write the Colt people when I get back,' he said weakly, slipping the gun away again. 'I think I'll tell them their factory loads do okay.

He righted the sled and straightened the dogs, calming them as best he could. He put MacSween back on top the tarpaulin and the old hunter said apologetically, 'Sorry, boy, but I think that tussle has opened my wound again.'

And a few miles away, the three pursuing men stopped and listened intently to the shots resounding through the ridge country. Then, glancing darkly at one another, they sped on . . .

ELEVEN

Kane thrust the sled through the snow with all his strength, the thought of the blood seeping from MacSween's reopened wound driving him on. The dogs toiled wearily and the sheathed rifle banged against his thigh uncomfortably, but at least it was getting colder, the loss of his snowshoes not as troublesome.

Yet it seemed to go slowly—*too* slowly for safety, and Kane was beside himself with worry. The shots fired while fighting the grizzly would carry like the wind in this narrow valley, acting as a stimulus on the pursuing killers. That Laverne was following was a fact Kane accepted with every taut nerve of his body. He tried not to show the panic and disappointment he felt every time the dogs tangled in their harness or the sled nosed into a snow bank, not wishing to frighten Valerie or the helpless Skinny.

Skinny panic?

The old trapper never lowered his carbine once. 'Let Laverne and his buzzards come,' he growled when his thigh was rebandaged and they were ready to go on again. 'This is the first time I've been sitting like I was a king, able to shoot while everybody else did the work!'

Kane stared at the frosty old head, bare now since he was wearing Skinny's coonskin cap. No matter how dangerous for himself, Kane thought, Skinny must be the one to remain alive and show the way to Beaver Creek. And Valerie—it would be tragic injustice for her to avoid a torturing death in Pembina Valley, only to meet it here in this frozen hell! *Hell*... People always considered hell as a place burning hot, but the hell he'd been visiting in the Dakota Territory was far below zero!

The sled clipped along at a decent speed whenever they

reached an open stretch of frozen bog, but every time they came to a ridge, no matter how high or low, it was a terrible hassle for Kane. They'd have to zig-zag up it, losing valuable time, the sled threatening to tip over any moment from the overweight.

Once, Skinny MacSween turned around and looked at Kane's thin-lipped, sweating face, and said with a weak smile: 'Too bad the bullet didn't go a bit higher, boy. You two could've made better time without me.'

'Shut up, you ancient bastard!' Kane panted, fighting the sled to keep it from tipping.

And once Kane stopped to listen intently. How far were they?

The sun was golden along the treetops, and seemed exceptionally warm to him. But that could have been because of his exertion, and his own heart was beating so loud, it was almost the only thing he could hear.

'Take a ten-minute break,' MacSween said, 'before you drop for good.'

The sled was standing at the rim of a wide, flat bog, long shadows casting from the nearby trees. But his eyes were focused across the bog, to the dark forest already behind them. He kicked the dogs, ordering them quiet, and in the hushed air he listened again ...

A faint, singing call came from the woods across the bog.

They were near ... and closing in!

Suddenly springing into action, Kane rousted the dogs and drove the sled into the woods, behind a thick, matted scrub. 'They're coming,' Kane said with fury. 'Valerie, stay here with Skinny. Take my revolver and use it if you have to. You can aim and shoot, can't you? Good! Don't go ... are you hearing me? Don't go from here no matter what happens to me. Skinny—you keep an eye on her!'

'Don't worry about us none, boy!' the old trapper said. 'Take cover behind that spruce back there, way up where our tracks show. We might be able to ambush them that way.'

'Right. And Skinny, you think you can call the dogs as if you were crossing a bog? You know, a little weaker all the time as if you're actually moving away.'

'I understand! Good luck to you, boy!'

Kane began running back the way they'd traveled, toward the large growth of spruce where protection was good. He turned around once, seeing Valerie standing beside *him* and not at the sled where she belonged! 'What the hell——?'

She gripped him tightly, kissing him fully on the lips. 'Be careful, Morgan. I couldn't bear it if——'

'Get back to Skinny!' he whispered fiercely, and thrust her from him. On he went then, jumping carefully behind the spruce so's not to leave tell-tale footprints in the snow. He unsheathed the spare Winchester, one he'd taken from the killers at MacSween's camp nights ago, and hunkered down among the branches as quietly as he could. He stared across the bog, hearing voices and the hum of the sled runners clearly across the level. His heart seemed to be stopping in his chest, a buzzing of anxiety ringing in his ears.

How many were there? Laverne and who else would be driving into the forest...?

The thought of the yelling, drunken Chippewas around the gallows in Pembina Valley sent a long shiver of apprehension through him. He gripped the Winchester harder and blew on the breech to try and keep it from freezing. Then he lay silently, fingering the extra ammunition in his jacket.

Skinny's voice rose ahead of him: 'On ... On, dogs, on...!' There was the faint singing of runners through snow; Kane had to smile lightly, thinking of how the old man must've gotten Valerie to push the sled. 'On ... On ...'

The voice faded gently, and all was quiet for a few moments. Then: 'Onnn ...' It sounded farther away now, MacSween turning to call in the other direction with his mitten over his mouth.

Then there was a creaking on the bog and snow sprinkled down from the spruce overhead. First one ... then two figures emerged from the woods across the frozen marshland ... and then Kane saw four, then five dogs plunge out into the open. Then the sled appeared, with two men.

Only two...

Kane felt a small amount of relief, thinking of the third white, the one he'd shot back in Pembina, still there with those infuriated Chippewas! The two pursuers were confident, no doubt, that they were enough for a single man and a near-naked girl. They had no reason to remember Skinny MacSween, or believe he was still alive...

The two men paused.

'On...' came the very soft call across the forest, MacSween's act sounding convincing even to Kane.

The men quickly unsheathed their rifles and started running for the spruce grove where Kane was hiding, their snowshoes swinging on their backs. Kane waited while they followed the sled trail, his left eye instinctively beginning to tic. He glanced at the woods across the bog again ... Weren't there any Indians along? Laverne must have begun the chase at once, before they could be sobered...

The distance shortened to eighty yards ... sixty ... fifty...

Kane raised the butt of his carbine, pressing his cheek against the freezing breech and sighting down the barrel. He aimed at the man on his right, not being able to tell because of their furs which was the dreaded Laverne.

Thirty ... twenty yards. Now Kane could see the frost around their anorak hoods, and the glint of the sun off their belts and rifles. Kane took a bead on that right-hand man's buckle and pulled the trigger.

He heard the resounding fire in his ears and saw the buckle explode, and before the man had time to fall, Kane had levered and was drawing a bead on the second man. Again the Marshal shot ... and the dark, hidden face in the anorak seemed to erupt like a volcano.

Kane stood, hearing the echo of his two shots echoing through the trees and between the high ridges. Then—another sound reached him, that of a shrill, hysterical cry for help.

'Kane! Oh, Morgan!'

Valerie!

Kane heard two sharp reports and then her yell again. He ran as fast as he could through the snow, leaping over and around the scrub, wincing instinctively as another shot was fired. And then he was back at the sled—and he saw to his horror that there had been three pursuing killers after all! *Three!* And the third man had detoured around, and was now standing belligerently behind MacSween, who wasn't able to turn around!

'The sled!' Kane called out as he charged into the small circle. 'Turn the sled over!'

The man turned, bellowing, and fired at Kane. The bullet zinged off a tree limb an inch from his face, but already MacSween was taking advantage of the diversion, throwing himself sideways off the sled. The man levered his Winchester and shot again.

Kane ducked behind a scrub, and the snarling killer fired again, raising a long scratch in the snow crust before him. Kane counted the number of shots he'd heard: six! The Winchester must be empty now!

But Kane's own rifle was jammed muzzle-down into the snow, forced there when Kane had dived for his life. When he brought it up, he realized that there was just as good a chance of it blowing his own head off as there was of shooting a bullet into the killer. The killer saw this too, and started for Kane, swinging the butt of his carbine like an axe. Kane thrust his hand inside his jacket for his revolver . . .

But his revolver wasn't there! Valerie had it!

Now the man was on him, and Kane recognized the fearsome scowl of Laverne! Kane rolled, and the heavy stock of the Winchester swung for his head, narrowly missing it and crunching down in the snow. Kane grabbed for it before Laverne could wrench it free, twisting it out of the other's grip, but losing it as well as he lost his own balance and fell back again.

'You bastard!' Laverne roared, and whipped out his long, wickedly sharp hunting knife. 'Now take a taste of this!'

Kane fumbled with his belt, his fingers slipping around his own knife. He pulled it with half-frozen numbness in his hand, holding it outward in awkward defense. As most gunmen, he felt a deep, abiding detest for cold, silent steel . . . and his enemy standing before him was an expert with knives!

'Morgan!' Valerie called. 'Oh God!'

'Get the sled righted!' Kane yelled, not taking his eyes off the wily Laverne. 'Get it up and get going!'

The vicious French-Canadian chuckled confidently and jumped toward him, the knife lightning-quick. Kane could not react in time, and the blade slit a long gash in his jacket, his own thrust easily parried by the hilt of Laverne's knife.

'Ah, you sweat!' Laverne hissed in his singing accent. 'Soon you'll be sweatin' blood!'

Laverne attacked again, and again a long rent was opened along the front of his fur coat. Kane twisted in desperation, trying to slash back against Laverne's arm ... but Laverne wasn't there any longer, moving away like the snake he was. Kane jerked, coming around, only to feel a strange, icy biting in his side, and stumbling back, he stared down at the foreign blade standing rigid in his flesh.

He stared at Laverne then, certain death releasing his fear and giving him reckless courage. He threw himself at the killer, yelling all his hatred and frustration, butting the man in the chest while his right arm whipped around in a classic roundhouse blow. The knife slid deep into Laverne's back. Kane, enraged more than the grizzly had been, kept a firm grip on his knife, yanking it out of Laverne and plunging it back in again, twisting it, sawing it, his mind beyond rationality.

The two stabbed men fell over in the snow, and Kane noticed the sharp, agonizing pain from Laverne's knife as it dislodged from his side in the tussle. He sprawled helplessly over his dead opponent, everything floating ... floating around him, warm and sticky...

Then *she* was there, quick and crying, helping him to his feet again, letting him fall against her for support. He groped one hand inside his jacket, feeling blood dribble over his palm, and he went unsteady again, clutching Valerie. Somehow she managed to get him to the sled, where he lay down beside MacSween, who was swearing a blue streak about not having been able to shoot Laverne.

'Sit down,' Skinny said. 'Sit down here, m'boy!'

They removed his jacket, and the chilly air rippled like an icicle across his fevered skin.

'Thank God,' Skinny said. 'Laverne's knife broke the skin and cut loose some of the flesh along your side. But it doesn't seem to have gone all the way in and pierced something vital! Mrs Fremont, hand me the knife, will you, and some straps ... What's the matter, aren't you well? You're looking like you might faint, Mrs Fremont ... Mrs Fremont? Oh Lord, there she went!'

The fire threw sharp relief against the tree trunks around them, and outside the tiny circle of flame, the forest was dark and forboding. What did it matter? They had warmth and food ... and they were alive!

Kane and MacSween were sitting side by side on the sled, looking at the long blonde hair of Valerie Fremont. She was sitting on a stump beside the fire, cooking dinner in a large-sized skillet, and the smell of meat and beans made everybody's mouth water.

'Ah,' MacSween said with a sign, 'smells almost as good as my own stew.'

Kane chuckled at the old trapper's boasting, feeling contented at the moment, his previous restlessness gone.

'No need to worry about the Chippewas,' MacSween said. 'When they sober up and see what they've done, they'll be running like scared rabbits all the way back to Saskatchewan, because they'll know Captain Faucher will be after them with a vengeance! They won't stop until they can pull the Northern Lights over them like a blanket!'

And a little later, Skinny rambled on: 'Peace to the forest again, and God sake's in time, too! I'd rather fight a mad grizzly a thousand times than be up against those blood-curdling Chippewas! Not to mention those bastards from Quebec.'

Kane sat, stiff and sore, enjoying the fire and the sight of Valerie's fine golden hair. He was amazed how well she had endured these horrible experiences and sudden deaths, but then he recalled a few other courageous women he'd known, especially years ago when he rode shotgun and guide on the wagon trains along the Oregon Trail. Hunger,

Indians, sickness . . . the wives and daughters of the settlers had buried many of their family beneath the strange land's earth, and then gone about their business with heavy heart but firmer resolve.

Once Oregon had been as much a border as the Pembina River, and people weren't that different, even when they spoke with a funny, clipped British accent.

And now, this evening, the three of them were suddenly thrown together, alone in a dead and frozen world, and the howling wolves they'd heard when leaving the bog didn't mean anything more to them than the crack of a frozen tree limb.

As Skinny had said when they'd stopped: 'This will be a camp to remember, folks, and if you don't feel about it the way I do, then you're both plumb crazy.'

It *was* an evening to remember. And remember they all did. Valerie Fremont would remember it long after she was married two years later in Winnipeg. Morgan Kane would retain warm memories for many years, recalling the frosty, beaded spruces and the blue, cold moon, and the shadows stealing around the snow-heavy scrub. Yes, and the gleam of the fire and the color of the pine when it sparked and flared up with pitch. He would always remember the feel of Valerie's hand, the taste of her lips, and the sound of her melodious voice when she said that dinner was ready . . . and it was as if she would have told him: 'Love, you saved me. Take me . . . I'm yours . . .'

It was quiet in the forest, and Skinny MacSween was able to sum it up in a single sentence, rare as that was for him.

'We won't reach Dawson's tomorrow or the next day,' he said wistfully, 'but by God, I'm looking forward to the smell of roach powder in that post of his!'

TWELVE

Laverne's knife had been dirty, and Kane's wound worsened and grew infected. Kane writhed with high fever, and Dawson was forced to cut open the wound and clean it. Dawson had placed him in a small room in the back of his post, which had mostly been used for stock and an occasional over-nighter, but Morgan Kane stayed there for weeks, fighting his sickness.

An old Crow brought him his food three times daily, and at regular intervals, the trappers and hunters of the area would drop by and talk with him. They told him the ice had broken on both the Cheyenne and Beaver rivers now, and that the snow was already melting while the gray goose soared overhead, northward.

Kane was in no particular hurry any longer. By April he could sit up and eat in the warm sunlight in front of the door. The nearby hills still had snow, and frost still stubbornly clung to the shadows and clefts between rocks, but most of the ground was bare and turning a velvety green.

As soon as MacSween's wounded thigh healed, he was down to say good-bye to Kane, saying he was on his way north again with the geese. Kane watched him go until he was only a little speck against the fresh green conifers, and he felt peculiarly sad and lonely with the loss of the old trapper.

Valerie came to see him on the fourth of April, and was pleased to find Morgan sitting in a chair in the yard. She was back in the bloom of health again, her cheeks rosy and her skin tanned, and her manner light and frisky as a colt's. She told him she'd been staying at a girl-friend's in Fargo, but that soon she would be off to Winnipeg, whenever the road was dry enough for a wagon and horse team. There, she said, she had arranged for a job in a hotel.

Kane asked her to sit down.

'You look very well, Morgan,' she said, arranging herself beside his chair.

'I feel well, Valerie. That old witch of a Crow wouldn't let me up until I could wrassle my way free.'

Valerie smiled. Morgan was still much thinner than he'd been when they'd met, but the spring sun had tanned him nearly as brown as she, and with his still-long black hair, he almost resembled a handsome Indian. The comparison caused her to shudder.

'Skinny has gone, I understand,' she said.

Kane nodded. 'He has to make his money, y'know.'

But the truth was, MacSween had refused the salary of a weekly fifty dollars they'd agreed upon, the old trapper waving the bills in Kane's face and snorting: 'Oh no, I don't get paid for having fun! Why, it was worth a coupla hundred dollars just to see you fight that grizzly!'

Kane looked at Valerie now, watching her open her jacket. She was wearing a gray, high-necked sweater beneath it, thin and thrusting over the mounds of her high, pointed breasts. Kane blinked, averting his eyes.

The sun gradually coasted over the western hills as they continued to converse, and when it was dusk and becoming chilly, he said to her: 'Come on in my little palace. You can have coffee, if you like, or a drink.'

'A drink sounds wonderful.'

She followed him inside the small room, looking around while Kane stoked the small stove into life. The sweet-smelling timber walls were chinked with growing moss, and the furniture was crude but sturdy, fashioned from axe and whittled with knife.

She remarked: 'What a cozy place, Morgan!'

'Well, Dawson had some of the men clean it out for me. I think they did a pretty fine job, all in all.' He took down a bottle of whiskey he'd had brought from Fargo, and poured two glasses with the decent brew, handing one to Valerie. In the light from the stove, her face was quiet, not showing the struggle of emotions seething inside of her.

She took a sip to calm her nerves and said: 'There's

something I want to tell you. You saved my life, and I can never forget it. You saved it several times, Morgan.'

Kane shuffled uncomfortably, not knowing what to say to that. Before he could think of a reply, she went on:

'I was married for four years, four long and mostly sad years. John was a kind man, and I liked him. But he was also a careful man, Morgan, and wanted the quiet life of a commandant. I don't fault him for his ways, because that's what he was and that's the way I married him ... but I'm telling you this so you ... you'll know. So you'll understand.'

'Yes,' Kane said, not understanding at all.

'When I first met you, it was such a change! John was mild, easy to like, and slow to anger. While you ... You're violent and strong and hard. Very hard and very independent.'

Kane slumped in a chair, mumbling with embarrassment.

'The night you undressed me, I first felt only shame, and ... yes, and fear. The intimacy between us was the exact opposite to what I'd been taught to believe in as right and proper.'

'Yes, that I understand,' he replied then, and did.

'It came to me later as I thought things over, that my life, especially with John, had always been ordered and neatly arranged. While yours has always been a constant struggle, forcing out of life what is necessary. You know, until I understood that, I was prepared to live my life alone, I was a widow, my husband gone and my home destroyed and most of my frinds dead—my world had ended, and I was willing to exist quietly in its memory. But not any longer. You showed me the will to carry on and carve something new. I'll go to Winnipeg and start over, dress not in widow's weeds but in something gay and bright. I'm still young, and I'm going to live my years to the hilt, and when I meet the man for me—and I will, I know I will—I will live for him.'

Kane emptied his glass and poured another quick drink for himself. He didn't care for where this conversation was heading.

'Had you been another sort of man, Morgan, with another profession not so deadly, I would have shamelessly followed you. You are a man easy to love but impossible to marry, and I must reconcile myself to this fact. I will take the next best. And I will . . . will stay here with you tonight. I want this night as a memory, just as that night we were all together in the forest.'

'You . . . You don't have to, Valerie.'

'Yes, I do. I have to finish what was started between us.'

Valerie Fremont rose from her chair then and locked the door to the room. She pulled the hand-woven curtains across the window and loosened her hair. It fell like a cascading shower of golden grain around her shoulders. Then she raised her hands to her bodice and began slowly, consciously unbuttoning her sweater. She paused, smiling with a woman's sensuality at the Marshal, and said to him:

'Will it bother your wound any?'

Kane smiled back at her, fingers shaking. 'Hell no.'

The woods were clean and the scent was fresh with the dew of morning. Spring had come, and the earth was drinking the melting snow greedily, only the darkest corners beneath the spruce still retaining patches of ice.

Morgan rode slowly along the riverbank. He was dressed in his own clothes, his heavy coat rolled and tied behind his saddle with his blankets and suitcase. A new Winchester protruded from the long holster against his leg, and around his hips was the belt which held his ammunition and Colt revolver. He rode, at peace with the world, up along Beaver Creek in the direction of Three Crow's cabin.

Snow still lay in several places, but already there were signs of beaver cutting the saplings and forming their woven houses in the stream, mending the winter's destruction.

Before he'd left Fargo, Kane had wired the Union Ranch in Fort Leavenworth. It was a long telegram, and it concluded with the fact that the affair was being handled in joint collaboration between the American authorities and the Canadian Mounties. Four Redcoats had ridden to

Dawson's, and Kane had spent a long night before the proper documents were filled out, signed, and the case was out of his hands. The young lieutenant from Winnipeg had told of Fort Pembina's commandant returning three days after the massacre, meeting a troop of farmers from the area who were coming back after their panicky flight. An orderly had been sent to Winnipeg, and a small army was put in the field to round up the Chippewa Indians. They'd discovered, as MacSween had prophesied, that the Indians were heading northward as fast as they could go. Yes, it was out of Kane's hands now ... or was it?

Kane moved on, traveling through what would be his final meeting with the Dakota country. The river bubbled, the sun burning with April intensity in a cloudless azure sky. Birds were deafening in the trees and rabbits hopped and skittered in all directions. Kane rode, shifting his weight in the saddle ... and then through the sprouting branches of the trees, he spied another horse farther up along the wooded trail.

A fur-dressed man squatted on the riverbank not far from the horse, where the river was shallow and gravelly. Kane opened his thin jacket and dismounted, snaking out his revolver as he moved toward the man, soundless on the spongy moss. He paused six yards away. The man's back was to him, and he seemed to be stooped over, doing something busily with a dishpan in the water.

Then Kane straightened, smiling, and walked toward the man. 'Hello, Skinny, you old reprobate!'

MacSween dropped the pan and swiveled around. His dark blue eyes were narrowed with suspicion until he recognized Kane, and then they twinkled in his leathery, bearded face.

They stared a long time at each other, and then MacSween said: 'I like you better in furskins, boy.'

Kane pulled out his Bull Durham pouch and rolled a cigarette. He continued to watch Skinny, no longer smiling, and Skinny's eyes dropped to the low-slung holster and the revolver that was in it.

'How did you find out?' he said, low and sharp.

'Something I overheard in Laverne's camp, up there in

Pembina Valley,' Kane replied. 'It didn't make any sense at first, all that stuff about when the ice had melted and so forth. What about you, Skinny?'

MacSween shrugged his shoulders. 'Never talked much about it,' he said. 'But back in seventy-four, I was one of the first to put his nose in the Black Hills, looking for gold. It was Sioux territory then, and I ended up getting thrown out by the cavalry. But I found some gold before I had to leave ... and then it occurred to me that the Garrison range is just north of the Black Hills, and part of the same formation. The river has its headwaters up there, so I put two and two together.'

'Laverne must have done that same figuring,' Kane said dryly. 'How did he get to suspect it?'

'Well, I've been thinking about that off and on. Might be because he was selling the Indians all that bad liquor, and they paid for it in gold.'

'Then there is gold here?'

MacSween nodded toward the river. 'I found a small poke in Three Crow's cabin, and so far I've gotten a little out of here. If you don't believe me, you can wash some out for yourself.'

'I believe you,' Kane said softly.

MacSween shook his head, turning away from the river. 'Most beautiful place in Dakota. Damned shame, it is.'

'What is?'

'Why, it'll be destroyed, everybody hot after the gold.' MacSween's voice rose now in anger. 'Why did Laverne have to ruin everything? Why did he have to kill and plunder all those people?'

'Laverne was Canadian, Skinny,' Kane reminded him. 'He couldn't live here, and could only manage to take the gold quietly, without anybody knowing he was this far south all the time. That meant getting rid of talkative Indians. It was bad luck for the Crows that Beaver Creek was such good hunting territory. Skinny, how much gold do you think is around this area?'

MacSween stroked his beard thoughtfully. 'Well, if I panned the whole summer, and fiddled with the traps only in winter, I imagine I could support myself. But it would be damned close, and nigh on impossible once the word was out.'

'Only you and I know it, Skinny,' Kane answered. 'Only you and I.'

MacSween frowned. 'But your report . . .?'

'I wrote that Laverne allied himself with the Chippewas to fight the Crows, who refused to pay him blackmail when he threatened them with war. Then when the Chippewas struck, he had to scare them to keep their mouths shut—and he killed their renegade leaders to make sure they couldn't tie him in to them. I think it was a pretty good story, and it'll stick.'

'All right,' MacSween said. 'I trust you, Morgan. And I want you to trust me, too. This is hunting country, boy—and this is the way it'll stay as long as I'm alive. Ah, how quiet and peaceful it is, and it's the way it should be. If you ever read in the newspapers that there's a gold rush around Beaver Creek, you can come up and collect my body.'

Kane dropped his cigarette and snuffed it out with his boot. 'It's an appointment, Skinny.'

'Hungry?'

'As a bear!'

MacSween laughed. 'I've some deer meat.'

Kane followed him into the woods. Behind them the river trickled on its merry way, glittering in the sun, and the beaver swam across the sparkling yellow granules that were washed across the pebbles and sand on the bottom, the gold that had always been there and would now remain untouched, winter, spring, summer, and autumn.

THE END

NO TEARS FOR MORGAN KANE

by LOUIS MASTERSON

David Kominsky was a Missouri farmer trying to eke out a living on land made barren by drought. 'Swinging' Johnson and his murderous band from Cross Bow ranch decided to lay claim to David's land—and crucified him to ensure he wouldn't dispute the matter. The Cross Bow gang had terrorised the countryside so thoroughly that the neighbouring farmers went in fear of their lives and the town marshal was a cowardly, useless creature. But by a lucky stroke of fate, Morgan Kane was not far away—waiting to pick up a train robber . . .

0 552 08923 0—**25p** T159

BETWEEN LIFE AND DEATH

by LOUIS MASTERSON

In Kane's early days as a Texas Ranger, he was given a tough assignment. He had to break a smuggling gang operating between Texas and Mexico. The traffic was in guns, and the gang leader was known as El Halcon—the hawk. Five rangers investigating the gun-running had lost their lives at Sierra Blanca, a little village south of El Paso. Kane set out for Sierra Blanca wondering if he would be the sixth man to die . . .

0552 08989 3—**25p** T160

RETURN TO ACTION *by* LOUIS MASTERSON

Kane was enjoying a life of contented peace in the mountains of New Mexico with his pretty young wife, Linda. He made a living by catching and selling half-wild horses. It was a frugal existence, but a happy one—until the brutal gang of killers arrived at his home. They murdered Linda and stole six of Kane's horses. From that day Kane was a man with only one purpose in life: to avenge his wife's murder. With his two Mexican friends, Rico and Casca, he set out in pursuit of the gang . . .

0 552 08990 7—**25p** T161

RIO GRANDE *by* LOUIS MASTERSON

Victor Brady wanted his wife back. He had a good idea who'd kidnapped her. The note said:

'You can fetch her for ten thousand dollars in gold. Come to the desert west of Guerrero and wait there . . .'

Brady set off at once for the town of Guerrero and there found Morgan Kane, living in a hovel with a Mexican girl. Kane was reluctant at first, but for a thousand dollars, he finally agreed to act as Brady's guide—in a desert swarming with bandits . . .

0 552 09048 4—**25p** T37